God's Got You

Looking for some truths about *how amazing you are?*

I've got something special just for you a
"Why Should I?"
sheet that knocks out all those false
accusations with Biblical truth!

Feeling fearful or
lost, like no one
understands you?

**Scan the QR
Code to Download
your sheet**

*Let God's truth sprinkle
you with love and value.*

Table of Contents

Cynthia Radtke

Christian

Devotional

for Teen Girls

60 + Faith Based Songs, Verses,

Quotes & Journaling Prompts

for Daily Bible Study

Table of Contents

Why it Matters

When I was in 5th grade, my mom started leaving little devotionals on my nightstand. I'd hop into bed, cozy up, and spot a new book. As I snuggled in, I'd grab it and read how a Bible verse connected to my life. I didn't realize then how much this would stick with me through my teen years—and even now.

Making time with God became my solid foundation. Nothing else in life—yours or mine—matters as much as that one-on-one time with Him.

My hope for you is that you'll dive into the Bible and discover just how much God loves you. This devotional is here to help you with that. It's written with love, so you can get to know the One who loves, cares, guides, heals, brings hope, and fills you with joy!

Starting Points

This devotional is super simple and all about pointing you to scripture.
You'll get:

- A key verse
- A short story
- Support verses
- Journal prompts that take you back to the support verses
- The "make it real" part. Putting what you've learned into action.
- A song to listen to! Music is an awesome way to worship, so turn it up, sing along, and praise God—He'll love it!
- A quote to get you thinking a little deeper and challenge you

As you dive deeper into getting to know God,
I want to share a simple but tremendous truth with you.
It's what a good friend frequently said to me. It was simply,
"Cynthia, God's got you!" ....and He always did!
He's got you too!
Enjoy and Grow!

Perfect Love

1 John 4:18 - "There is no fear in love. But perfect love drives out fear, because fear has to do with punishment. The one who fears is not made perfect in love."

Imagine you're starting a new school year. The hallway is packed with people, and every step you take feels like eyes are on you. You feel that fear in your chest and wonder, "Will they like me? Will I fit in?" The fear of rejection makes you want to run away. You try to keep your head down, but deep inside you long to be noticed for who you are.

This fear can creep into friendships, social media, or even how you view yourself. But the Bible reminds us that God's love is so perfect, it chases away our fears. God's love isn't based on how you look, act, or perform. He loves you fully just as you are. When you allow his love to fill your heart, the fear of not being good enough fades away. **God's perfect love makes you fearless.**

More Verses

Romans 8:38-39 NIV - "For I am convinced that neither death nor life, neither angels nor demons, neither the present nor the future, nor any powers, neither height nor depth, nor anything else in all creation, will be able to separate us from the love of God that is in Christ Jesus our Lord."

Isaiah 41:10 NIV - "So do not fear, for I am with you; do not be dismayed, for I am your God. I will strengthen you and help you; I will uphold you with my righteous right hand."

How do these verses apply to you? What's the message?

1. **From Romans 8:38-39,** write a few things that cannot separate us from the love of God.

2. **From Isaiah 41:10,** why should we not fear? What are two things God promises to do for us?

Gratitude Jar for God's Love

Place a gratitude jar in your room. Whenever you feel grateful for God's love or support, write it down and put the note in the jar. Review these notes weekly or monthly to see how God's love remains constant in your life.

Music for Your Heart

Take a moment and listen to
"Perfectly Loved"
by Rachael Lampa ft. TobyMac

Something to Remember

"Fear will always knock at your door. Just don't invite it in for dinner. And for heaven's sake, don't offer it a bed for the night." - *Max Lucado*

The Power of God's Word

Psalm 119:11 - "I have hidden your word in my heart that I might not sin against you."

You're scrolling through social media when a post pops up. It's one of those things that's hard to resist clicking on even though you know it's not helpful or encouraging. The temptation to see what everyone's talking about is strong. But then you remember a verse from your morning devotion—God's word is in your heart and mind, reminding you of what's true and good. In moments of temptation, his word becomes your shield, guiding you to make choices that honor him.

When you memorize scripture and keep it close, it's like carrying a flashlight in the dark. God's word lights your path, helping you avoid stumbling blocks and giving you strength when things get tough. The more you keep his word in your heart, the more it shapes your thoughts and actions.

More Verses

Psalm 19:7-8 NIV - "The law of the Lord is perfect, refreshing the soul. The statutes of the Lord are trustworthy, making wise the simple. The precepts of the Lord are right, giving joy to the heart. The commands of the Lord are radiant, giving light to the eyes."

Colossians 3:16 NIV - "Let the message of Christ dwell in you richly, as you teach and admonish one another with all wisdom through psalms, hymns and songs from the Spirit, singing to God with gratitude in your hearts."

How do these verses apply to you? What's the message?

1. **Based on Psalm 19:7-8,** what does the Law of the Lord do for your soul? What do His statutes make you? How do his precepts affect your heart?

2. **In Colossians 3:16** name three things you are encouraged to do with the Word of God?

Positive Reminder

Write down these verses on a few sticky notes and place them in areas you frequently look at, such as your study desk, bathroom mirror, or the back of your phone.

Music for Your Heart

Take a moment and listen to
"This is our God"
by Phil Wickham

Something to Remember

"The Bible will keep you from sin, or sin will keep you from the Bible."
- *Dwight L. Moody*

Trust in God's Protection

Psalm 3:3 - "But you, Lord, are a shield around me, my glory, the one who lifts my head high."

It's one of those days at school that feels more like everything is going wrong than right. First, a pop quiz in math catches you off guard, and you're not sure you did well. Then, during lunch, you find out there's a rumor going around about you, twisting your words from a conversation days ago. By the time the final bell rings, you're emotionally drained, dreading the conversations with your family where tensions have been high lately.

Heading home, you feel the day's troubles weighing you down. Then you recall Psalm 3:3, a verse you found during your time with God. It reminds you that he is right there with you, acting as your shield. Thinking of God as your protector lightens your load, and you feel reassured that you're not dealing with life's messes by yourself.

More Verses

Psalm 18:2 NIV - "The Lord is my rock, my fortress and my deliverer; my God is my rock, in whom I take refuge, my shield and the horn of my salvation, my stronghold."

Ephesians 6:16 NIV - "In addition to all this, take up the shield of faith, with which you can extinguish all the flaming arrows of the evil one."

How do these verses apply to you? What's the message?

1. Wow, so many ways God protects you. List a few mentioned in **Psalm 18:2.**

2. **In Ephesians 6:16,** what do you use to fight against the evil one?

Personalized Bookmark

Design a bookmark featuring Psalm 3:3 along with symbols that represent protection and safety, like a guardian angel or a shield. Use it in your daily reading to keep the verse close.

Music for Your Heart

Take a moment and listen to
"Good Morning"
by Mandisa & TobyMac

Something to Remember

"God is most glorified in us when we are most satisfied in him." - *John Piper*

Embracing Change Gracefully

Isaiah 43:19 - "See, I am doing a new thing! Now it springs up; do you not perceive it? I am making a way in the wilderness and streams in the wasteland."

Your family has just moved to a new city, far from the friends and community you've grown up with. The prospect of starting over is daunting, and you feel a mix of sadness and resistance. But as you unpack in your new room, you find a photo album filled with memories of past adventures and achievements, reminding you of how you've gone through change before.

You begin to see this move not as a loss, but as an opportunity for new beginnings. You decide to get involved. You join a local youth group and volunteer at a community center, where you meet others and start forming new friendships. With each step, you discover that accepting change can lead to surprising joys and growth, and that God is present, creating new paths in what seemed like an unknown wilderness.

More Verses

Ecclesiastes 3:1 NIV - "There is a time for everything and a season for every activity under the heavens."

Philippians 4:6-7 NIV - "Do not be anxious about anything, but in every situation, by prayer and petition, with thanksgiving, present your requests to God. And the peace of God, which transcends all understanding, will guard your hearts and your minds in Christ Jesus."

How do these verses apply to you? What's the message?

1. What does it mean to you that God has planned different seasons for your life according to **Ecclesiastes 3:1?**

2. How do you get God's peace in your new situation according to **Philippians 4:6-7?**

Adventure Bucket List

Create a "New Adventure Bucket List" for your new city. Add fun ideas like visiting a park or joining a youth event. Pick one to try this week and invite someone new to join you. Snap a picture during the adventure and share it as a reminder that God is making something new in your life!

Music for Your Heart

Take a moment and listen to
"New Day"
Danny Gokey

Something to Remember

"We can't change the past, but we can start a new chapter with a happy ending." - *Billy Graham*

Cultivating Self-Worth

Psalm 34:5 - "Those who look to him are radiant; their faces are never covered with shame."

Lately, you've been feeling down about yourself, comparing your looks and achievements to those you see on social media. It's easy to feel like you're not good enough, that you're somehow lacking. Why not talk to someone about how you're feeling, perhaps even opening up to your mother, father or someone you trust.

You could explore together Psalm 34:5 and discuss how shifting your focus to God, rather than social media or peers for validation, could change your perspective. They could share stories from when they were teens to show self-doubt is normal, but knowing how God sees you can build your confidence.

More Verses

Romans 8:37 NIV - "No, in all these things we are more than conquerors through him who loved us."

I John 3:1 NIVa - "See what great love the Father has lavished on us, that we should be called children of God! And that is what we are!"

How do these verses apply to you? What's the message?

1. Who does **Romans 8:37** tell us we are more than conquerors through?

2. As you look in **I John 3:1,** what does this verse say about how much God loves us, and what does that make us?

Share & Encourage

Maybe with friend or family member, create a board filled with positive affirmations from scripture to celebrate your unique qualities as seen through God's eyes.

Music for Your Heart

Take a moment and listen to
"Flawless"
by MercyMe

Something to Remember

"Your value doesn't decrease based on someone's inability to see your worth."
- *Anonymous*

Goals, Doodles & Thoughts

Use this space to write or draw about any key points, questions, or goals.

_____

_____

_____

_____

_____

_____

_____

_____

_____

_____

_____

_____

_____

_____

_____

The great thing about faith in God is that it keeps a man undisturbed in the midst of disturbance!

- *Notes on Isaiah*

Leading with Compassion

Colossians 3:12 - "Therefore, as God's chosen people, holy and dearly loved, clothe yourselves with compassion, kindness, humility, gentleness, and patience."

You've recently been elected as the president of your school's community service club. The position comes with expectations and responsibilities that sometimes feel overwhelming. During one of the meetings, you notice a member who seems discouraged because their ideas aren't being heard.

After the meeting you decide to pull them aside and listen to their concerns and ideas. This act of compassion leads to a new project that becomes one of the club's most successful programs, benefiting the local shelter. God prompted your leadership style to help create a supportive and collaborative environment, making the club not only more effective but also a place where members feel valued and heard. Where is God prompting you?

More Verses

1 Peter 3:8 NIV - "Finally, all of you, be like-minded, be sympathetic, love one another, be compassionate and humble."

Philippians 2:4 NIV - "Not looking to your own interests but each of you to the interests of the others."

How do these verses apply to you? What's the message?

1. In what ways have you been sympathetic towards someone this week? If you can't think of a time, re-read **I Peter 3:8** and ask God to give you an opportunity to do this.

2. According to **Philippians 2:4,** whose interests are we supposed to look out for?

Small Act of Kindness

If your friend has a big project due or a lot of homework, surprise them with their favorite coffee or snack to give them a little boost of energy. Or, if you know they've been stressed about an upcoming exam, offer to study together and help quiz them on the material. If they've been feeling overwhelmed, you could even help organize their locker or lend a hand with something they've been putting off. These acts of kindness show that you're paying attention to their needs and want to lighten their load in any way you can.

Music for Your Heart

Take a moment and listen to
"With Every Act of Love"
by Jason Gray

Something to Remember

"People don't care how much you know until they know how much you care."
- *Theodore Roosevelt*

Finding Worth in God's Eyes

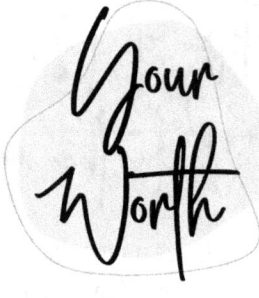

Zephaniah 3:17 - "The Lord your God is with you, the Mighty Warrior who saves. He will take great delight in you; in his love he will no longer rebuke you but will rejoice over you with singing."

You've been trying out for the lead role in your school's spring play, and despite your best efforts, you're given a "supporting" part. You feel a mix of disappointment and inadequacy, questioning your abilities and your worth.

In reading Zephaniah 3:17, God sees you as valuable and delights in you, not based on your roles or achievements, but simply because you are his. Looking at it differently, this helps boost your performance by shifting your focus from seeking recognition to giving your best effort. When you stop worrying about being in the spotlight, you free yourself from unnecessary pressure, allowing your true abilities to shine. Plus, when you're not caught up in trying to outshine others, you can actually enjoy what you're doing and feel proud of your efforts!

More Verses

Psalm 139:14 NIV - "I praise you because I am fearfully and wonderfully made; your works are wonderful, I know that full well."

1 Peter 2:9 NIV - "But you are a chosen people, a royal priesthood, a holy nation, God's special possession, that you may declare the praises of him who called you out of darkness into his wonderful light."

How do these verses apply to you? What's the message?

1. How does **Psalm 139:14** say you were made, and what does that reveal about how God sees you?

2. Based on **I Peter 2:9,** what are you encouraged to do as His special possession? How will you do this today?

Verse Voice Memo

Record yourself reading the verses for today in Zephaniah, Psalms and I Peter. Listen to these recordings each morning or before going to bed as a personal reminder of these powerful truths. This can help start or end your day with a strong sense of God's love and your worth in his eyes.

Music for Your Heart

Take a moment and listen to
"Priceless"
by King & Country

Something to Remember

"You are valuable because you exist. Not because of what you do or what you have done, but simply because you are." - *Max Lucado*

Leadership in Everyday Life

Joshua 1:9 - "Have I not commanded you? Be strong and courageous. Do not be afraid; do not be discouraged, for the Lord your God will be with you wherever you go."

At the start of the semester, you notice some of the younger students looking totally lost—just like you felt a few years ago. Joshua 1:9 pops into your head, and you feel like maybe you should do something to help. But the idea of starting a group? Organizing isn't your strong suit and its overwhelming. What if no one supports the idea? What if you let everyone down?

Still, you decide to go for it. You talk to your friends and the school counselor, and they're all in. Their enthusiasm gives you courage, but as you start planning, the challenges hit hard. Trying to figure out schedules, setting up meetings, and keeping everything straight? It's harder than you thought. At one point, you're so stressed you want to quit. But every time you feel like you're drowning, you ask God for help, and somehow, you keep going.

When the group finally starts, it's not perfect, but it works. The younger students seem less nervous, and your friends are stepping up as leaders too. You realize it's not about being the most organized or having all the answers—it's about showing up, trusting God, and doing your best. And as the group grows, so does your confidence that God can use even your messy efforts to make a big difference.

More Verses

Philippians 2:3-4 NIV - "Do nothing out of selfish ambition or vain conceit. Rather, in humility value others above yourselves, not looking to your own interests but each of you to the interests of the others."

James 3:13 NIV - "Who is wise and understanding among you? Let them show it by their good life, by deeds done in the humility that comes from wisdom."

24

How do these verses apply to you? What's the message?

1. Whose interests are you supposed to be focused on according to **Philippians 2:3-4?**

2. What are two traits **James 3:13** says you should show when you're around others?

Serve Quietly

Do good things for others without seeking praise or attention. Find someone who is struggling with their homework. Spend t me with them after school, explaining the answers without expecting any praise. You're helping because you care, not for attention or recognition.

Music for Your Heart

Take a moment and listen to
"Less Like Me"
by Zach Williams

Something to Remember

"Leadership is not about being in charge. It is about taking care of those in your charge." - *Simon Sinek*

Value Beyond Achievements

Galatians 3:26 - "So in Christ Jesus you are all children of God through faith."

You're sitting at the kitchen table with your latest report card spread out in front of you. The grades are lower than you expected, and you feel a sinking sense of disappointment. You brace yourself for your parents' reaction, worried that they'll be upset or disappointed in you too. But when they sit down to discuss it, their reaction surprises you. They acknowledge your efforts and remind you that these grades aren't a reflection of your worth. They talk about strategies for improvement, sure, but more importantly, they stress that your value isn't tied to these grades.

Instead of beating yourself up over a less-than-perfect GPA, you start to see learning as a journey of growth. You get involved in a peer tutoring group not just to boost your grades, but to help others too, reinforcing the idea that everyone has unique strengths and struggles. It's about lifting each other up, not just pushing yourself forward.

More Verses

1 Samuel 16:7 NIV - "But the Lord said to Samuel, 'Do not consider his appearance or his height, for I have rejected him. The Lord does not look at the things people look at. People look at the outward appearance, but the Lord looks at the heart."

Ephesians 2:10 NIV - "For we are God's handiwork, created in Christ Jesus to do good works, which God prepared in advance for us to do."

How do these verses apply to you? What's the message?

1. According to **1 Samuel 16:7,** what does God look at instead of outward appearance?

2. According to **Ephesians 2:10,** God created you to do GOOD works because you are his what? Shift your perspective on self-worth - your value is defined by God!

Social Media Post

Post about Ephesians 2:10 and give yourself a little reminder: you're God's masterpiece! Yep, you were custom-made with a purpose, designed for good things. So go ahead and own how amazing you are—you're crafted by the ultimate Creator! Share it on your social media to boost your self-worth and encourage your friends to do the same.

Music for Your Heart

Take a moment and listen to
"Gold"
by Britt Niccle

Something to Remember

"Our worth is not determined by our wins or losses but by our willingness to learn from them and move forward." - *Mandy Hale*

Living Righteous

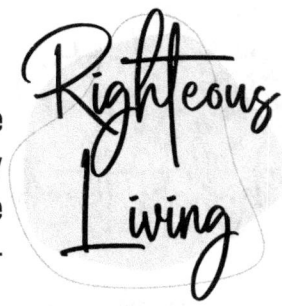

Romans 12:2 · "Do not conform to the pattern of this world, but be transformed by the renewing of your mind. Then you will be able to test and approve what God's will is – his good, pleasing and perfect will."

It's a Friday night, and your friends are texting about hanging out. You get the invitation, but you know they're planning to go somewhere that doesn't feel right to you. There's a pull in your heart—you don't want to miss out, but you also know it's not where you should be. That's when the verse you read earlier in the day comes to mind. God's word reminds you of what's good and true. Even when no one is watching, it guides you in making the right choices.

When you hide God's word in your heart, it becomes like your inner GPS, steering you away from temptation and guiding you toward decisions that honor him.

More Verses

Ephesians 6:13-14 NIV - "Therefore, put on the full armor of God, so that when the day of evil comes, you may be able to stand your ground, and after you have done everything, to stand. Stand firm then, with the belt of truth buckled around your waist, with the breastplate of righteousness in place."

Proverbs 21:3 NIV - "To do what is right and just is more acceptable to the Lord than sacrifice."

How do these verses apply to you? What's the message?

1. **In Ephesians 6:13-14,** what does the armor of God do for us? What are the two parts mentioned in the verse and what do each of them do?

2. What is more acceptable than sacrificing to God according to **Proverbs 21:3?**

Accountability Group

To tackle peer pressure, form an accountability group with a couple close friends with the same values. Set clear rules, create a group chat for support, and have a specific check in day to discuss challenges and victories.

Music for Your Heart

Take a moment and listen to
"Speak Life"
by TobyMac

Something to Remember

"God calls us to live righteous lives, not because we're perfect, but because we're his." - *Jennie Allen*

Goals, Doodles & Thoughts

Use this space to write or draw about any key points, questions, or goals.

_____

_____

_____

_____

_____

_____

_____

_____

_____

_____

_____

_____

_____

_____

_____

_____

"Special" is a word that is used to describe something one of a kind, like a hug
or a sunset
or a person who spreads love with a smile or a kind gesture.

"Special" describes people who act from the heart and keep in mind the hearts of others.

"Special" applies to something that is admired and precious and which can never be replaced.

"Special" is the word that best describes you.

- Teri Fernandez

True Friends

Proverbs 18:24 - "One who has unreliable friends soon comes to ruin, but there is a friend who sticks closer than a brother."

You're hanging out with your group of friends after school, and suddenly, the conversation turns negative. Someone starts gossiping about a classmate, who is a friend of yours, and you feel stuck. You don't want to be involved, but you also don't want to be the one to say something and be left out. It's in moments like these that you discover the true meaning of friendship.

A true friend isn't just someone who sticks around when things are easy—they're the ones who encourage you to live for God and do what's right biblically. Jesus is that friend who never lets you down. He shows you what it means to be loyal and loving, guiding you to choose friends who lift you up and inspire kindness towards others.

More Verses

I Thessalonians 5:11 NIV - "Therefore encourage one another and build each other up, just as in fact you are doing."

Proverbs 27:9 NIV - "Perfume and incense bring joy to the heart, and the pleasantness of a friend springs from their heartfelt advice."

How do these verses apply to you? What's the message?

1. What are two things you can do to strengthen your friendships according to **I Thessalonians 5:11?**

2. In **Proverbs 27:9,** what kind of advice would a friend offer?

Gratitude Swap

Grab some of your friends, agree to write down three things you appreciate about each other. Swap lists with one other and discuss the qualities you all shared. It's a meaningful way to express love and remind one another of your worth in both your friendships and in God's eyes.

Music for Your Heart

Take a moment and listen to
"Friend of God"
by Israel Houghton

Something to Remember

"A true friend encourages us, comforts us, supports us like a big easy chair, offering us a safe refuge from the world." - *Francine Rivers*

Owning Your Words

Psalm 19:14 · "Let the words of my mouth and the meditation of my heart be acceptable in your sight, O Lord, my rock and my redeemer."

You're in the middle of a heated debate in your history class, discussing a complex topic that has everyone stirred up. In the heat of the moment, you find yourself snapping harshly at a classmate whose opinion differs from yours. The words leave your mouth before you can catch them, and immediately, you regret it. The room goes quiet, and you can see the hurt in your classmate's eyes.

That night, as you think about everything that happened during the day, you open your journal to write and come across Psalm 19:14, a verse you highlighted earlier. The words hit you differently this time. You realize how easy it is to overlook your own mistakes and not others, especially when you're feeling emotional. Motivated by the verse, you decide that tomorrow you'll apologize to your classmate. Owning up to your mistakes is the first step to making sure they don't control you.

More Verses

Proverbs 10:19 NIV - "Sin is not ended by multiplying words, but the prudent hold their tongues."

Proverbs 12:18 NIV - "The words of the reckless pierce like swords, but the tongue of the wise brings healing."

How do these verses apply to you? What's the message?

1. What does **Proverbs 10:19** tell us about the importance of speaking less? What do the prudent do?

2. How do you think you can bring "words of healing" to others as it says in **Proverbs 12:18?**

Admit a Mistake

Here's a task to challenge yourself: The next time you make a mistake, take a deep breath and admit it. Whether it's with a friend, family member, teacher, or whoever, go to the person, acknowledge what you did wrong, and sincerely apologize. This small action shows maturity and builds trust in your relationships. Reflect on why the mistake happened and what you can learn from it. Admitting your faults helps you grow and keeps your connections strong and healthy.

Music for Your Heart

Take a moment and listen to
"Words"
by Hawk Nelson

Something to Remember

"Reflect before you act, this gives control over impulsive sins"
- *John Piper*

Choosing a Career Path

Proverbs 16:3 · "Commit to the Lord whatever you do, and he will establish your plans."

You're in your junior year of high school, and everyone seems to be asking, "What are you planning to do after you graduate?" You've always been interested in art, but your parents are encouraging you to pursue something more "practical" like business. It's overwhelming to think about making a decision that could shape the rest of your life.

On career day, you talk with professionals from different jobs. You meet a graphic designer who combines creativity and business, which gives you an idea. Could this be a way to use your love for art in a stable career? You decide to look into it more, ask your art teacher for advice, and pray for God's guidance. Excited, you realize, God can use your talents in ways you hadn't thought of before.

More Verses

Jeremiah 29:11 NIV - "For I know the plans I have for you," declares the Lord, "plans to prosper you and not to harm you, plans to give you hope and a future."

Psalm 37:5 ESV - "Commit your way to the Lord; trust in him, and he will act."

How do these verses apply to you? What's the message?

1. What plans does God have for your future according to **Jeremiah 29:11?**

2. As you commit AND trust your plans to the Lord, what does **Psalm 37:5** tell you he will do?

What's Next?

Based on what you're interested in, try job shadowing or interning to get a feel for different jobs. Look into options like college, trade school, or taking a gap year after high school for more experience. Set some goals and make a simple plan to help you move forward.

Music for Your Heart

Take a moment and listen to
"Thrive"
by Casting Crowns

Something to Remember

"God doesn't call the qualified, he qualifies the called." - *Mark Batterson*

Courage to Stand

II Timothy 1:7 - "For the Spirit God gave us does not make us timid, but gives us power, love and self-discipline."

Heather and Lisa sat on the couch, scrolling through social media. Lisa stopped on a video mocking Christians. "Can you believe people still believe this stuff? It just doesn't make sense anymore," she said.

Heather hesitated. Faith wasn't something they'd ever talked about. But she felt a nudge: Speak up. Remembering the verse God had given her about not being timid and that he gives her power, love, and self-discipline, she took a deep breath. "I get why some people feel that way, but my faith means everything to me. It's helped me through so much."

Lisa looked surprised. "Like what?" Heather shared how trusting God gave her peace during her dad's illness. Lisa listened quietly, her tone softening.

Sharing your faith with loved ones can be intimidating, but God gives you the courage to speak with kindness and love. Even if their response isn't immediate, trust God to nurture the seed you've planted.

More Verses

Romans 1:16 NIV - "For I am not ashamed of the gospel, because it is the power of God that brings salvation to everyone who believes: first to the Jew, then to the Gentile."

I Peter 3:15 NIV - "But in your hearts revere Christ as Lord. Always be prepared to give an answer to everyone who asks you to give the reason for the hope that you have. But do this with gentleness and respect."

How do these verses apply to you? What's the message?

1. What does **Romans 1:16** say about the power of the gospel and who it can save?

2. According to **I Peter 3:15**, what should you always be ready to do and how should it be done?

Sharing Faith with Love

This week, take a bold step and share your faith on social media. Start by choosing either a short personal story about how your faith has helped you or a favorite Bible verse like II Timothy 1:7. If you go with the story, think of a time when trusting God gave you peace or strength. If you choose the verse, write about why it matters to you.

Add a meaningful photo, like a sunset or your Bible, and trust that God can use your words. Don't worry about reactions—respond with kindness and stay calm if someone disagrees. Your goal is to plant a seed and share your faith with love.

Music for Your Heart

Take a moment and listen to
"You Say"
by Lauren Daigle

Something to Remember

"God is using your present circumstances to make you more useful for later roles in his unfolding story." - *Lysa TerKeurst*

Navigating Peer Pressure

1 Corinthians 10:13 - "No temptation has overtaken you except what is common to mankind. And God is faithful; he will not let you be tempted beyond what you can bear. But when you are tempted, he will also provide a way out so that you can endure it."

You're at a party with some school friends when someone suggests playing a game that makes you uncomfortable. The pressure to join in is intense—everyone else seems eager, and you don't want to be the only one to say no. You feel torn between wanting to fit in and knowing that participating goes against your values.

Remembering 1 Corinthians 10:13, you muster the courage to politely decline, suggesting an alternative game instead. To your surprise, a couple of other friends who also seemed hesitant join you, grateful for someone taking the lead. This experience not only strengthens your resolve to stand by your beliefs but also shows you the impact of leading by example in uncomfortable situations.

More Verses

James 4:7 NIV - "Submit yourselves, then, to God. Resist the devil, and he will flee from you."

Proverbs 1:10 NIV - "My son, if sinful men entice you, do not give in to them."

How do these verses apply to you? What's the message?

1. How does **James 4:7** direct you to be free from the devils' temptations?

2. Very directly **Proverbs 1:10** tells you to do what when sinful people tempt you?

Start a Prayer Group

Grab a few friends who share your faith and start a prayer group. You can meet up or start a group chat where you pray for each other, especially when you're feeling tempted. If someone needs extra support, they can ask for prayers, and everyone backs them up. It's a great way to help each other stay strong and make good choices.

Music for Your Heart

Take a moment and listen to
"Crazy People"
by Casting Crowns

Something to Remember

"Character is doing the right thing when nobody's looking." - *J.C. Watts*

Goals, Doodles & Thoughts

Use this space to write or draw about any key points, questions, or goals.

_____

_____

_____

_____

_____

_____

_____

_____

_____

_____

_____

_____

_____

_____

_____

You must think of your time with God as the most important part of your day — it's where you recharge, get inspired, and tackle life from His direction. Make it a top priority no matter who else wants your time for it will impact everything else you do.

- Adapted from David Wilkerson

Endurance Through Trials

James 1:12 - "Blessed is the one who perseveres under trial because, having stood the test, that person will receive the crown of life that the Lord has promised to those who love him."

Sarah felt like her whole world was falling apart. Her dad had passed away unexpectedly last year, and the pain still felt fresh. To make things worse, she recently got a failing grade on a big test, and her boyfriend broke up with her out of nowhere. Everything seemed to be going wrong, and she didn't know how to handle it all. She questioned why God was allowing so much pain in her life.

One night, Sarah was reading her Bible and found James 1:12. It hit her that struggles are just part of life and God sees everything she's going through. The verse reminded her that if she keeps trusting God during tough times, he has something good waiting for her—His strength, comfort, and a reward. Even though nothing in her life had changed yet, Sarah felt more at peace. She realized that God was with her in every trial, helping her grow through it all.

God's Word shows us that going through tough times is part of our faith journey. Hard things like losing someone, failing, or going through a breakup can feel like too much. But these moments are chances to lean on God and trust His plan. He promises a reward for staying strong in our faith. It's not about pretending everything's fine but believing that God can bring good out of our struggles.

More Verses

Romans 8:28 NIV - "And we know that in all things God works for the good of those who love him, who have been called according to his purpose."

2 Corinthians 4:17 NIV - "For our light and momentary troubles are achieving for us an eternal glory that far outweighs them all."

How do these verses apply to you? What's the message?

1. A promise is stated in **Romans 8:28.** What is it? Put your name in the verse and claim it!

2. How does **2 Corinthians 4:17** remind us of God's purpose in our trials, similar to **James 1:12?**

Be Real

When you're going through a tough time, don't hold back from telling God how you feel. Be honest with him about your fears, frustrations, or doubts, just like you would with a friend. God wants to comfort and guide you through your pain. Opening up to him helps you feel less alone and brings peace, knowing he's with you through it all. Talking to God regularly can keep you strong, even when life feels overwhelming.

Music for Your Heart

Take a moment and listen to
"Hills and Valleys"
by Tauren Wells

Something to Remember

"Hardships often prepare ordinary people for an extraordinary destiny."
- *C.S. Lewis*

God's Throne is Accessible

Revelation 4:11 - "You are worthy, our Lord and God, to receive glory and honor and power, for you created all things, and by your will they were created and have their being."

Maya sat on her porch watching as the sunset created a painted sky full of beautiful shades of pink and orange. She had just come home from a youth conference where they had talked about God's throne and how amazing it is to be able to approach him. Sitting there, she couldn't help but think about how huge and powerful God is—he created the entire universe, every star, and yet he still wanted to hear from her. It made her feel both small and amazingly loved.

That night, Maya read Revelation 4:11, which reminded her that God is worthy of all glory and honor. She was struck by how incredible it is that, despite his greatness, he invites her to come before his throne. This wasn't just any throne—it was the throne of the Creator of everything! Maya prayed, not out of desperation or a need for something, but simply to give God praise for who he is.

More Verses

Psalm 95:6 NIV - "Come, let us bow down in worship, let us kneel before the Lord our Maker."

Hebrews 12:28 NIV - "Therefore, since we are receiving a kingdom that cannot be shaken, let us be thankful, and so worship God acceptably with reverence and awe."

How do these verses apply to you? What's the message?

1. How does **Psalm 95:6** remind you of God's worthiness of our worship, just like in **Revelation 4:11?**

2. Why should we be thankful to God according to **Hebrews 12:28?**

Create a Worship Playlist:

Make a playlist of worship songs that focus on God's glory! Start by choosing songs like "What a Beautiful Name" by Hillsong Worship, or "How Great is Our God" by Chris Tomlin. Set aside time daily to renew yourself and fill yourself with worship! Whether in the morning, during a break, or before bed, as you listen, sing your heart out to God! Also, think about the lyrics while you listen, using this time to connect with God and give him praise for who he is.

Music for Your Heart

Take a moment and listen to
"Glorious Day"
by Passion

Something to Remember

"The God who made the universe, with all its grandeur and wonder, made you and delights in you. What an amazing thought!" - *Max Lucado*

Laughter and Enjoying Life

Proverbs 17:22 - "A cheerful heart is good medicine."

Sophie and her friends spent the afternoon at a local park, soaking up the sunshine. As they were finishing their picnic, a street performer dressed as a mime approached them. His exaggerated movements and pretend box routine were funny, but when a squirrel decided to investigate his prop bag, things got hilarious. The squirrel hopped in and out of the bag while the mime pretended to argue with it, all without saying a word. Sophie and her friends were laughing so hard they could barely breathe.

As Sophie walked home, she thought about how much better she felt after laughing so much. She realized that God's gift of joy is one of the best ways to refresh her spirit. Laughter is like sunshine for the soul—it can turn a good day into a great one and make ordinary moments feel special. She thanked God for the ability to laugh and share joy with her friends.

More Verses

Nehemiah 8:10 NIV - "The joy of the Lord is your strength."

Proverbs 15:13 NIV - "A happy heart makes the face cheerful."

How do these verses apply to you? What's the message?

1. In **Nehemiah 8:10,** what is our strength? Even in hard times, it is a strength from God!

2. When your heart is happy, what will you feel inside according to **Proverbs 15:13?**

Spread Cheer

Send a funny meme or text to a friend who needs a smile, or leave a kind note for someone at school. Even small gestures, like helping your sibling with their chores or sharing a laugh, can brighten someone's day—and yours too!

Music for Your Heart

Take a moment and listen to
"Every Good Thing"
by The Afters

Something to Remember

"There's no greater joy than being in the will of God." - *David Jeremiah*

Strength in Weakness

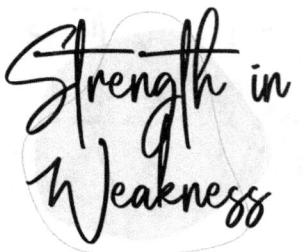

2 Corinthians 12:9 - "But he said to me, 'My grace is sufficient for you, for my power is made perfect in weakness.' Therefore, I will boast all the more gladly about my weaknesses, so that Christ's power may rest on me."

Your day begins with a daunting task: you have to lead the class in a math exercise, even though math has never been your strong suit. Then you have to give a class presentation which stirs up your anxiety about public speaking. Making things worse, you forgot your notes at home. At lunch, you try joining a new club to make friends but feel awkward and out of place. Later, a misunderstanding leads to an argument with your best friend, adding emotional stress to an already chaotic day.

In those moments, God reminds us that it's okay to be weak. In fact, our weakness is an opportunity for his power to shine. When you stop relying on your own strength and start leaning on God's grace, you find a strength that goes beyond what you could ever do on your own. It's okay to admit you need help because God's grace is more than enough.

More Verses

Philippians 4:19 NIV - "And my God will meet all your needs according to the riches of his glory in Christ Jesus."

Isaiah 40:29 NIV - "He gives strength to the weary and increases the power of the weak."

How do these verses apply to you? What's the message?

1. Where do our needs get met according to **Philippians 4:19?**

2. In **Isaiah 40:29,** what does the Lord give to the weary? What does he give to the weak?

Strength Finder

Think about three times this week when you felt totally drained or stressed—maybe a hard test, a fight with a friend, or too much on your "to-do" list. Write down what happened and how God helped, even in small ways, like giving you strength or sending someone to encourage you. Then, share one of those stories with a friend who might need to hear it. Show them how God can show up when things feel tough.

Music for Your Heart

Take a moment and listen to
"Even If"
by MercyMe

Something to Remember

"God will meet you where you are in order to take you where he wants you to go." - *Tony Evans*

Overcoming Fear

Isaiah 41:10 - "So do not fear, for I am with you; do not be dismayed, for I am your God. I will strengthen you and help you; I will uphold you with my righteous right hand."

Lately, the atmosphere at home has been tense. Your parents have been going through a tough time, and their arguments seem to escalate every night. This constant conflict makes studying and sleeping difficult, leaving you feeling stressed, alone and afraid. One evening, as voices rise again downstairs, you put on your headphones to drown out the noise, but the anxiety and fear are hard to escape.

In moments like this, God's presence is your strength. He doesn't just tell you not to be afraid; He promises to be with you, to strengthen you, and to help you through it. When you face scary situations, remember that God is right there with you, holding your hand and giving you the courage to face your fears.

More Verses

Psalm 34:4 NIV - "I sought the Lord, and he answered me; he delivered me from all my fears."

II Timothy 1:7 NKJV - "For God has not given us a spirit of fear, but of power and of love and of a sound mind."

How do these verses apply to you? What's the message?

1. In order to be delivered from our fears, what does **Psalm 34:4** tell us to do?

2. In **II Timothy 1:7,** name the three things that God has given us?

Faith vs. Fear

Make a Fear vs. Faith chart. The goal is to help you replace fear with faith using scripture.

Draw two columns, list your fears on one side, and match them with Bible verses that address each fear on the other. For example, if you're afraid of failure, write Philippians 4:13 ("I can do all things through Christ") in the faith column. Display the chart where you can see it, and use this chart when fear starts to sneak up on you. This will remind you of God's promises and strengthen your faith as you face challenges.

Music for Your Heart

Take a moment and listen to
"The Breakup Song (Fear You Don't Own Me)"
Francesca Battistelli

Something to Remember

"Replace what you don't know about the future with what you do know about God." - *Christine Caine*

Goals, Doodles & Thoughts

Use this space to write or draw about any key points, questions, or goals.

_____

_____

_____

_____

_____

_____

_____

_____

_____

_____

_____

_____

_____

_____

_____

_____

For a saint to love as God loves is the most practical thing imaginable.

- David Wilkerson

Trusting God's Timing

Psalm 27:14 - "Wait for the Lord; be strong and take heart and wait for the Lord."

You've been praying for something big—maybe healing for a family member, fixing a broken friendship, or landing a role in the student council. But time's ticking—days, weeks, or even months—and it seems like nothing's happening. It's hard not to get frustrated when you don't see answers right away.

God calls us to trust his timing, especially when it doesn't match with our expectations. Maybe there's a reason the answer hasn't arrived yet, or maybe God is preparing you for something even better. **His timing is perfect, and when we wait with trust, we grow stronger in faith.**

More Verses

Lamentations 3:25 NIV - "The Lord is good to those who hope in him, to the one who seeks him."

Romans 5:5 NIV - "And hope does not put us to shame, because God's love has been poured out into our hearts through the Holy Spirit, who has been given to us."

How do these verses apply to you? What's the message?

1. Hope in the Lord, ...it is stretching – as you seek him, how does he treat you according to **Lamentations 3:25**? Think of a few ways he shows that to you now?

2. What a gift we have...what does **Romans 5:5** tell us we get? Two things actually, what are they? Take a second and thank the Lord for these two gifts and trust him!

Prayer Journal

Write down your prayers and thoughts every day this week. This helps you keep track of your feelings and any changes in what you're waiting for. Reviewing your entries can show you how God s working in your life over time. Plus, you can look back and see the answered prayers – be encouraged!

Music for Your Heart

Take a moment and listen to
"I Speak Jesus"
by Charity Gayle

Something to Remember

"Patience in God's timing isn't passive; it's active faith, believing that he's working in ways we can't see yet." - *Allie Beth Stuckey*

The Power of Encouragement

Proverbs 18:21 - "The tongue has the power of life and death, and those who love it will eat its fruit."

At school, you overhear some girls talking behind someone's back. They're saying mean things, and you can tell that the person they're talking about is really hurt. It's easy to get caught up in gossip or say something we don't mean when we're upset, but God's Word reminds us that our words have power.

Whether you're with friends, at home with family, or participating in youth group activities, you have the ability to lift others up or tear them down. Choose to speak positively, to encourage others, and to remind your friends and family of God's love. Words can heal or hurt, and God calls us to use them for good. It's not an option!

More Verses

Ephesians 4:29 NIV - "Do not let any unwholesome talk come out of your mouths, but only what is helpful for building others up according to their needs, that it may benefit those who listen."

Colossians 4:6 NIV - "Let your conversation be always full of grace, seasoned with salt, so that you may know how to answer everyone."

How do these verses apply to you? What's the message?

1. By sharing things about others that are positive, what impact does this have
   on them and others according to **Ephesians 4:29?**

2. How should our conversation be according to **Colossians 4:6?** What does
   the verse say are the benefits of obeying this request from God?

Response Strategies

It's okay to think differently and stand up for what's right. When you do, keep your tone kind and respectful. Have good reasons ready for why you disagree or why you are speaking up. If you're feeling really emotional, take a moment to calm down before you respond. Letting yourself cool off can help you speak more clearly.

Music for Your Heart

Take a moment and listen to
"What You're Worth"
by Mandisa

Something to Remember

"Encouragement is oxygen to the soul." - *John Piper*

Leading by Example

1 Timothy 4:12 - "Don't let anyone look down on you because you are young, but set an example for the believers in speech, in conduct, in love, in faith, and in purity."

You're at youth group, and the leader is asking for volunteers to help plan an upcoming event. You feel a nudge in your heart to step up, but then a voice inside tells you, "You're too young. Let someone older do it." It's easy to think that because you're a teenager, you can't make a big impact.

But Paul's message to Timothy reminds you that age doesn't limit your ability to lead. Whether you're at home with your siblings, at school with friends, or in church with your youth group, God can use you to set an example for others. Your love, faith, and actions speak volumes, and God can do incredible things through you, no matter your age.

More Verses

Matthew 5:16 NIV - "In the same way, let your light shine before others, that they may see your good deeds and glorify your Father in heaven."

Titus 2:7 NIV - "In everything set them an example by doing what is good. In your teaching show integrity & seriousness."

How do these verses apply to you? What's the message?

1. When you let the light of Jesus shine in you, what happens according to **Matthew 5:16?**

2. As you work with others, teaching them, encouraging them, what three things does **Titus 2:7** say to do and show?

God's Checklist

Create a chart in your journal or one to hang on your wall. List things God has put on your mind to do, to lead or even to create. What has God placed on your heart? Remember, he has chosen you specifically for this! Before you begin each one, take a moment to pray for strength, direction, and wisdom. As you work through your list, mark off completed items and jot down a celebration about it!! Don't forget to thank God for his guidance in the achievements you've made.

Music for Your Heart

Take a moment and listen to
"Be The Change"
by Britt Nicole

Something to Remember

"You don't have to be a certain age to make a difference. God can use you exactly where you are." - *Carter Conlon*

Forgiveness in Family

Ephesians 4:32 - "Be kind and compassionate to one another, forgiving each other, just as in Christ God forgave you."

You and your sibling got into a huge fight over something small—maybe they borrowed your favorite shirt without asking or didn't clean up their mess in your shared room. It's so easy to hold onto anger and frustration, especially with family. But then you remember how much God has forgiven you.

Forgiveness doesn't mean what happened is okay, but it means letting go of the bitterness and choosing to show the same grace God has shown you. Family can be tough, but God calls us to forgive and love each other through it. When we forgive, we reflect God's heart and restore relationships.

More Verses

Matthew 6:14-15 NIV - "For if you forgive other people when they sin against you, your heavenly Father will also forgive you. But if you do not forgive others their sins, your Father will not forgive your sins."

Colossians 3:13 NIV - "Bear with each other and forgive one another if any of you has a grievance against someone. Forgive as the Lord forgave you."

How do these verses apply to you? What's the message?

1. This topic can be a tough one! In **Matthew 6:14-15** what does God say he will do if we forgive others? What will happen if we choose not to forgive others?

2. We are called not to just forgive others, but to also do what according to **Colossians 3:13?** What does this verse say about the way we are to forgive? Pretty amazing!!! He will empower you to do it! Just obey!

Feel & Forgive

Today, start by recognizing and accepting how you feel about what happened—whether it's anger, sadness, or confusion. It's important to know that these feelings are normal. At the same time, learn what forgiveness really means – to understand that forgiving someone isn't about saying what they did is okay, but about choosing to let go of the anger so you can move forward.

Music for Your Heart

Take a moment and listen to
"Forgiveness"
by TobyMac

Something to Remember

"Forgiveness is unlocking the door to set someone free and realizing you were the prisoner." - *Max Lucado*

63

Rooted in Faith

Colossians 2:6-7 - "So then, just as you received Christ Jesus as Lord, continue to live your lives in him, rooted and built up in him, strengthened in the faith as you were taught, and overflowing with thankfulness."

Chloe's storm hit when her parents decided to separate. What!!?? The news shattered her world, leaving her feeling lost, broken and questioning God. She struggled with anger, sadness, and fear of what would happen. Chloe turned to God. She prayed for peace in her heart and wisdom for her parents. Through tear-filled nights and moments of doubt, she trusted that God had a plan, even in the pain.

In the midst of her parents' separation, Chloe chose to stay rooted in her faith in Christ. Despite her pain and doubts, she didn't allow her circumstances to define the attitude in her life. She turned to God, praying and claiming his word about being "built up" and "strengthened in faith." Offering God thankfulness, even in tough times shatters the darkness.

More Verses

Psalm 1:3 NIV - "That person is like a tree planted by streams of water, which yields its fruit in season and whose leaf does not wither—whatever they do prospers."

Ephesians 3:17-18 NIV - "So that Christ may dwell in your hearts through faith. And I pray that you, being rooted and established in love, may have power, together with all the Lord's holy people, to grasp how wide and long and high and deep is the love of Christ."

How do these verses apply to you? What's the message?

1. In **Psalm 1:3** we are compared to a tree that is by "streams of living water." What does it yield? What happens to ts appearance? What happens to it overall? That is what you can and will do as your roots go deep into the living water of God's word.

2. Wow, what great love God has for yoɹ in **Ephesians 3:17.** What is one way you can see the love of God in your life right now? Name it and thank Him for it!

Make a Tree

Start by sketching a tree in your journal, on a poster, or even on your wall (just check with your parents first ♡). Whenever something good happens, write it on the leaves. Draw a Bible at the base with roots around it, showing you're like a tree growing strong in God's words. Each new leaf you add represents growth and how God is actively shaping your life.

Music for Your Heart

Take a moment and listen to
"Up"
by Tauren Wells

Something to Remember

"Stay planted in the bed of faith. Your roots will grow in such depth that nothing can move you." - *Babbie Mason*

Goals, Doodles & Thoughts

Use this space to write or draw about any key points, questions, or goals.

_____

_____

_____

_____

_____

_____

_____

_____

_____

_____

_____

_____

_____

_____

_____

_____

Jesus, I like what I am because it was Your idea. Help me to find adventure in my uniqueness, and not want to be what someone else is. God, if I lose sight of the fun of being me, then Your dreams of what I can be in the world will die. Always help me to remember, that this is Your way of being creative.

- Ann Kiemel Anderson

Supporting Each Other in Faith

Hebrews 10:24-25 · "And let us consider how we may spur one another on toward love and good deeds, not giving up meeting together, as some are in the habit of doing, but encouraging one another—and all the more as you see the Day approaching."

Your younger sibling has been struggling with their faith, questioning a lot about what they believe and why. You've noticed them pulling away from family prayers and church activities. It's easy to feel worried or even judgmental, but as a family, this is a time to draw closer, not pull away.

Opening up about your faith with your sibling can bring you closer and help you both grow. Try sharing some of your own doubts and how you've handled them, or even suggest reading a devotional together. Connecting with Christ goes beyond just showing up at church—it's about being real with him and each other's experiences and supporting each other through all the twists and turns.

More Verses

1 Thessalonians 5:11 NIV · "Therefore encourage one another and build each other up, just as in fact you are doing."

Galatians 6:2 NIV · "Carry each other's burdens, and in this way, you will fulfill the law of Christ."

How do these verses apply to you? What's the message?

1. What two things does **I Thessalonians 5:11** tell us to do with other believers?

2. How do you follow the law of Christ in **Galatians 6:2?** Who do you know right now that needs this kind of support? Text them or give them a call.

Reflect and Do

Think of two people that you know need some encouragement. Give them a call and plan a time to go over to their place or meet up somewhere. Offer them what God puts on your heart, a verse, a small gift, just time listening. Pray with them before you leave. Set a goal to accomplish this within two weeks.

Music for Your Heart

Take a moment and listen to
"Walk With Jesus"
by Consumed by Fire

Something to Remember

"Encouragement is the kind of expression that helps someone want to be a better Christian, even when life is rough." - *Billy Graham*

Valuing Parents' Guidance

Ephesians 6:1-3 · "Children, obey your parents in the Lord, for this is right. 'Honor your father and mother'—which is the first commandment with a promise—'so that it may go well with you and you may enjoy long life on the earth."

Lately, it feels like your parents just don't get where you're coming from. They question everything—from the friends you choose to how you like to spend your free time—and it can feel like they're always on your case. This makes you frustrated and like they're trying to control you.

When you choose to stop and think about it, you realize they're probably doing this out of love and from their own experiences. They want to keep you from making mistakes and are trying to protect you. Remembering this can help you see their rules not just as restrictions but as their way of looking out for you. This understanding could help improve how you talk and connect with them.

Be open to sharing your thoughts respectfully and to hearing theirs. This can help bridge the gap between your experiences and their concerns.

More Verses

Proverbs 1:8-9 NIV · "Listen, my son, to your father's instruction and do not forsake your mother's teaching. They are a garland to grace your head and a chain to adorn your neck."

Colossians 3:20 NIV - "Children, obey your parents in everything, for this pleases the Lord."

How do these verses apply to you? What's the message?

1. How does following your parents' guidance as suggested in **Proverbs 1:8-9** impact you? Look up what these two things represent and how they affect you as a person.

2. So, in **Colossians 3:20,** when are we to obey our parents? And why?

Chat with the Parents

Think of a few things in your life where it feels like you and your parents are speaking different languages—like when they just don't get why something is so important to you. Jot them down, not to point fingers, but to help explain how you feel. Then, pick a good time to chat. Share your thoughts with kindness, and don't forget to really listen to their side too. Who knows? It could turn into a chance to grow closer and maybe even laugh about it later!

Music for Your Heart

Take a moment and listen to
"Control"
by King + Country

Something to Remember

"The most important thing that parents can teach their children is how to get along without them." - *Frank A. Clark*

Provision in Every Need

2 Corinthians 9:8 - "And God is able to bless you abundantly, so that in all things at all times, having all that you need, you will abound in every good work."

*As the school year progresses, you find yourself increasingly worried about college tuition. Despite having a part-time job and saving carefully, the figures seem discouraging. Discussions at home about finances often end in stress, adding to your anxiety about the future. During a particularly challenging week, you attend a youth group meeting where the leader shares 2 Corinthians 9:8, discussing God's promise to provide for ALL of our needs, **abundantly!***

This verse inspires you to readjust your approach to your financial worries. Instead of allowing anxiety to overwhelm you, you start researching scholarships and financial aid options, praying for guidance and provision. Hanging onto the biblical promise, you also organize a meeting with your school's guidance counselor, who helps you identify potential scholarship opportunities you hadn't considered.

More Verses

Matthew 6:31-33 NIV - "So do not worry, saying, 'What shall we eat?' or 'What shall we drink?' or 'What shall we wear?' For the pagans run after all these things, and your heavenly Father knows that you need them. But seek first his kingdom and his righteousness, and all these things will be given to you as well."

Psalm 23:1 NIV - "The Lord is my shepherd, I lack nothing."

How do these verses apply to you? What's the message?

1. What practical steps can you take to trust in God's provision from **Matthew 6:31-33?**

2. In **Psalm 23:1,** notice how David says, "The Lord is MY shepherd." What makes this personal connection special?

Stop and Remember

Take a few minutes to think about all the ways God has taken care of you. Write them down and thank him for always being there. Now think about how he's helped your family, your friends, or even your youth group—seriously, he's been busy! Take a moment to thank him! Keep trusting that his promises are always true.

Music for Your Heart

Take a moment and listen to
"I'm So Blessed"
by CAIN

Something to Remember

"Trust God's timing. It's better to wait a while and have things fall into place than to rush and have things fall apart." - *Sadie Robertson Huff*

Perfect Peace

Isaiah 26:3 - "You will keep in perfect peace those whose minds are steadfast, because they trust in you."

During final's week at school, everything feels like it's caving in. You're juggling homework, projects, and studying. Socially, it feels like your friends are drifting away, each of them wrapped up in their own stress, barely talking, and not hanging out like they used to. You're lying awake at night, tossing and turning.

One morning, desperate for some peace, you open your Bible and come across Isaiah 26:3. As you read the words, it hits you—peace doesn't come from having it all together, but from keeping your mind focused on trusting God, regularly.

Feeling a sense of hope, you make a decision. Instead of letting the stress take over, you choose to prioritize your relationship with God. You carve out a few minutes each day for prayer and reading the Bible. With each day, you start to feel calmer inside and that sense of anxiety starts to loosen its grip.

This new approach doesn't just help with the pressure of exams or friends—it teaches you that trusting God brings peace, and that peace helps you handle whatever comes your way.

More Verses

John 14:27 NIV - "Peace I leave with you; my peace I give you. I do not give to you as the world gives. Do not let your hearts be troubled and do not be afraid."

Philippians 4:6-7 NIV - "Do not be anxious about anything, but in every situation, by prayer and petition, with thanksgiving, present your requests to God. And the peace of God, which transcends all understanding, will guard your hearts and your minds in Christ Jesus."

How do these verses apply to you? What's the message?

1. **John 14:27** tells you that God gives you what? What should your heart be like?

2. When you are in a tough situation what are the steps outlined in **Philippians 4:6-7.** What promise do you receive if you follow these?

Identifying the Time

Set aside 10 to 15 minutes a day to read a short passage from the Bible. Invite a friend or family member to join you. Challenge each other to stick with it and share what you've learned. As it becomes a habit, gradually increase your reading time and have fun discussing your thoughts together.

Music for Your Heart

Take a moment and listen to
"Peace Be Still"
by Hope Darst

Something to Remember

"Peace is not the absence of trouble, but the presence of Christ."
- *Sheila Walsh*

The Joy of Friendship

Proverbs 17:17 - "A friend loves at all times, and a brother is born for a time of adversity."

Ana and her best friend, Yara, had a friendship filled with laughter, fun, and countless inside jokes. From movie marathons and making silly Instagram posts, to camping under the stars at summer camp, they had experienced amazing moments. But they had also faced hard times together. When Ana's parents divorced and when Yara lost her grandmother, the girls had prayed together and encouraged one another with Bible verses. They even survived middle school drama!

One afternoon at the park, Yara smiled and said, "I'm so glad we're friends. I don't know what I'd do without you!" Ana grinned and replied, "Me too! God has truly blessed us with this friendship."

Proverbs 17:17 reminds us that true friends are there for each other, no matter what. Ana and Yara knew that their friendship was a gift, not just for the fun moments but for those times when they needed support and love. They both felt that their friendship was special because it reflected the kind of love God calls us to show—unconditional and constant.

More Verses

Proverbs 27:17 NIV - "As iron sharpens iron, so one person sharpens another."

Romans 12:10 NIV - "Be devoted to one another in love. Honor one another above yourselves."

How do these verses apply to you? What's the message?

1. How does **Proverbs 27:17** connect with the idea of friends making each other stronger?

2. Friendship has some very specific characteristics in **Romans 12:10,** what are the two ways you are to treat one another? Which one would be more difficult for you to do? Well, then, pray for a chance to practice it with someone this week.

Thanks "My Friend"

Take a moment to write a note to a close friend, thanking them for being there for you. Mention a specific time they helped you or made you feel special. Let them know how much their friendship means to you. Send it as a text, or in person, or leave it somewhere they'll find it. It doesn't have to be long—just from the heart!

Music for Your Heart

Take a moment and listen to
"Friend in Jesus"
by CAIN

Something to Remember

"Allow God to continually soften your heart so that it beats for what his heart beats for—people." - *Christine Caine*

Goals, Doodles & Thoughts

Use this space to write or draw about any key points, questions, or goals.

_____

_____

_____

_____

_____

_____

_____

_____

_____

_____

_____

_____

_____

_____

_____

_____

Faith never knows where it is being led, but it loves and knows the One Who is leading.

- My Utmost for His Highest

Substance Abuse

Ephesians 4:2 - "Be completely humble and gentle; be patient, bearing with one another in love."

Sheila noticed her bestie Cathy wasn't her usual self lately - no more Instagram sharing or coffee hang outs. When she accidentally saw messages on Cathy's phone about addiction, her heart sank. That night, she opened her Bible app. Reading Ephesians 4:2, she realized true friendship meant being patient and loving, even in the hard times. Cathy needed a friend who would stick by her through this, not judge her. It wouldn't be easy, but Sheila knew God was calling her to help carry this burden.

The verse shows us that we are not meant to walk through life alone. When our friends are struggling, whether it's with substance abuse or something else, God calls us to help carry their burdens. This doesn't mean you have to fix everything, but it does mean offering support, love, and prayer. Helping a friend in a tough situation is one way to live out Christ's love.

More Verses

Galatians 6:1 NIV - "Brothers and sisters, if someone is caught in a sin, you who live by the Spirit should restore that person gently. But watch yourselves, or you also may be tempted."

John 15:12 NIV - "My command is this: Love each other as I have loved you."

How do these verses apply to you? What's the message?

1. In **Galatians 6:1,** what should we be careful about when we try to help someone else? What kind of attitude does God want us to have when someone is caught in a mistake?

2. In **John 15:12** what is the command that God gives you? List a couple of people he wants you to love.

Trusted Adult

Don't try to handle this on your own. Reach out to a trusted adult, like a parent or youth leader, who can guide you. They may offer advice, connect your friend to resources or even intervene if necessary. At the same time, stay close to your friend—listen, offer support, and let them know you care. Sometimes just being there makes a huge difference. But remember, it's important to make sure your friend gets the help they need.

Music for Your Heart

Take a moment and listen to
"Rescue"
by Lauren Daigle

Something to Remember

"You have never really lived until you have done something for someone who can never repay you." - *John Bunyan*

Resilience in Growth

James 1:2-3 - "Consider it pure joy, my brothers and sisters, whenever you face trials of many kinds, because you know that the testing of your faith produces perseverance."

Hailey had a rough week. She didn't make the soccer team, her grades were slipping, and her best friend moved away. It felt like everything was falling apart, and she didn't know how to cope. One evening, after crying alone in her room, Hailey's mom came in, sat beside her, and shared James 1:2-3 with her. She explained that life's struggles don't define us—how we choose to face them does. Hailey realized that strength wasn't about pretending everything was fine but trusting God to carry her through the hard moments.

As Hailey kept trusting God through prayer and reading her Bible, she started feeling stronger and noticed changes in her life. She didn't get overwhelmed by every problem anymore. Instead, she felt calmer, knowing that each challenge was making her stronger in her faith. Pushing through tough times gave her new hope, and she began to see difficulties not only as roadblocks, but as chances to grow closer to God and find out more about his plans for her.

More Verses

Romans 5:3-4 NIV - "Not only so, but we also glory in our sufferings, because we know that suffering produces perseverance; perseverance, character; and character, hope."

Philippians 4:13 NIV - "I can do all this through him who gives me strength."

How do these verses apply to you? What's the message?

1. According to **Romans 5:3-4** what does suffering produce? What does perseverance produce? What does character produce?

2. God gives us strength so we can do what? Look back at **Philippians 4:13.** What a promise!

Challenges List

Reflect on what's been weighing you down, whether it's school, friendships, family, or personal fears, and write them down in a journal or a "notes app". Pray about each challenge, asking God for guidance and strength. Read aloud the scriptures from above to strengthen your trust.

Music for Your Heart

Take a moment and listen to
"Overcomer"
by Mandisa

Something to Remember

"God does not waste a hurt." - *Rick Warren*

Bible Study Together

Matthew 18:20 - "For where two or three gather in my name, there am I with them."

Cathy loved hanging out with her friends at youth group, but when Bible study rolled around, she'd sometimes feel a little anxious. What if she didn't know the answers? What if someone asked a question she couldn't figure out? But one night, as they gathered to dive into God's Word, Cathy realized it wasn't about knowing it all. She heard her friends sharing their thoughts and being open about their own questions and struggles. As they prayed together and supported one another, she saw how much more meaningful Bible study was when it became a safe space to grow, connect, and experience God's presence.

Bible studies with friends aren't just about chatting—they're moments to lift each other up in your walk with God. As you read his Word, open up about what's in your heart, and pray as a group. You create deep connections that help you grow stronger in your faith. Joining a small group helps us feel God's love and learn more about his Word. It gives us the confidence to live it out with support.

More Verses

Ecclesiastes 4:9-10 NIV - "Two are better than one, because they have a good return for their labor: If either of them falls down, one can help the other up. But pity anyone who falls and has no one to help them up."

Colossians 3:16 NIV -"Let the message of Christ dwell among you richly as you teach and admonish one another with all wisdom through psalms, hymns, and songs from the Spirit, singing to God with gratitude in your hearts."

How do these verses apply to you? What's the message?

1. According to **Ecclesiastes 4:9-10** what specific help can a friend provide when you fall down?

2. In **Colossians 3:16,** what are three musical ways we can teach and encourage each other with God's Word?

Doing Good

Set a goal of doing something "good" each day this week. Pray and ask God who it should be for and what you are to do. Watch, listen for him to direct you. Challenge a friend to do it with you!

Music for Your Heart

Take a moment and listen to
"The Blessing"
by Kari Jobe & Cody Carnes

Something to Remember

"When we study God's word together, it's like having multiple flashlights in a dark room - we see so much more together." - *Alisa Childers*

More Than Your Struggles

Psalm 139:14 - "I praise you because I am fearfully and wonderfully made; your works are wonderful; I know that full well."

Harper dreaded English class. Reading aloud made her stomach churn, and the words on the page seemed to jump around. By the time she finished a sentence, the class had moved on. Her friends didn't mean to hurt her, but their quiet giggles when she stumbled made her want to disappear. No matter how much she practiced at home, reading never got easier, and frustration would quickly set in. She began to believe, "I'll never be as smart as them."

When you believe God made you wonderfully, even with your challenges, it changes how you see yourself. Instead of shame, you trust that God has a purpose for every part of your life, including the hard times. You don't have to be perfect for God to love or use you. Your worth comes from him, not from how well you perform. As you lean on him, you'll find strength, knowing he's shaping your story in his perfect way.

More Verses

I Peter 5:7 NIV - "Cast all your anxiety on him because he cares for you."

II Corinthians 12:9 NIV - "But he said to me, 'My grace is sufficient for you, for my power is made perfect in weakness.' Therefore, I will boast all the more gladly about my weaknesses, so that Christ's power may rest on me."

How do these verses apply to you? What's the message?

1. **1 Peter 5:7** tells us to give all our worries to God. Why does the verse say we can do this?

2. According to **2 Corinthians 12:9,** in our weakness, we are to rely on God's what? Why boast about your weakness – what is God's promise of power going to do?

Wonderfully Made

In your journal, list three things that make you feel "wonderfully made" by God. The next time you feel discouraged, pray **Psalm 139:14** over yourself, asking God for the strength you need to keep going.

Music for Your Heart

Take a moment and listen to
"Until Grace"
by Tauren Wells

Something to Remember

"God does not call the qualified, he qualifies the called." - *A.W. Tozer*

Your Identity in Christ

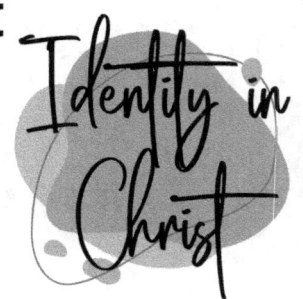

1 Peter 2:9 - "But you are a chosen people, a royal priesthood, a holy nation, God's special possession, that you may declare the praises of him who called you out of darkness into his wonderful light."

Addison, Kinsley, and Claire sat around their kitchen table one afternoon, working on a project for their youth group. The girls were making posters about their unique qualities as part of an activity designed to help them reflect on who they are in Christ. Addison, who loved music, spoke up, "I feel so lucky that God gave me the talent to play guitar. Whenever I play worship songs, I feel so connected to him, like I'm using the gift he gave me to show him how much I love him." Kinsley, who was a natural encourager, nodded, "I know! I've realized that God has made me a great listener, and I love being able to help my friends when they're going through tough times." Claire, always the creative one, added, "And I think it's pretty cool that God gave me the talent to paint. I feel like I'm reflecting his beauty through my art."

The girls all smiled, realizing how special they were in God's eyes—not because of what they could do, but because they were his chosen daughters. Each of their talents was a reflection of his love and creativity. They weren't just ordinary—they were God's royal, chosen people, created to bring glory to him through their unique talents.

More Verses

Ephesians 2:10 NIV - "For we are God's handiwork, created in Christ Jesus to do good works, which God prepared in advance for us to do."

Romans 12:6-8 NIV - "We have different gifts, according to the grace given to each of us. If your gift is prophesying, then prophesy in accordance with your faith; if it is serving, then serve; if it is teaching, then teach; if it is to encourage, then give encouragement; if it is giving, then give generously; if it is to lead, do it diligently; if it is to show mercy, do it cheerfully."

How do these verses apply to you? What's the message?

1. What are we created to do with the gifts God has given us according to **Ephesians 2:10?**

2. How can you use the unique gifts God has given you like in **Romans 12:6-8,** to serve others and glorify him?

Gifts Put to Work

This week - offer to use one of your talents to serve someone else, whether that's playing music at church, encouraging a friend, or creating something beautiful to inspire others.

Music for Your Heart

Take a moment and listen to
"Who I Am"
by Blanca

Something to Remember

"You are not an accident. You are a creation of God, and he has a plan and a purpose for your life. You are loved, valued, and chosen by him." - *Joyce Meyer*

Goals, Doodles & Thoughts

Use this space to write or draw about any key points, questions, or goals.

_____

_____

_____

_____

_____

_____

_____

_____

_____

_____

_____

_____

_____

_____

_____

_____

_____

A personal insult becomes an opportunity for a saint to reveal the incredible sweetness of the Lord Jesus!

- My Utmost for His Highest

Tough Times

Proverbs 3:27 - "Do not withhold good from those to whom it is due, when it is in your power to act."

Alyssa's heart sank when she got the text: her best friend, Kayla, had been in a terrible car accident and was now paralyzed from the waist down. Alyssa felt overwhelmed with sadness and fear. The girl who had once been the most active person she knew—dancing, running, always on the go—now couldn't even stand on her own. Alyssa didn't know what to say when she visited Kayla in the hospital. She felt helpless, not wanting to upset her by bringing up the accident, but also not knowing how to act "normal."

Alyssa tried to stay cheerful around Kayla, but deep down, she knew her friend was struggling. One day, while praying, Alyssa read Proverbs 3:27, "do good when it's in your power to act," and realized being there for Kayla wasn't about fixing things or making her smile—it was about walking through the tough times with her.

On her next visit, Alyssa asked Kayla how she was really feeling. Kayla opened up, and Alyssa just listened. It was hard, but Alyssa knew her presence made a difference. She realized that real friendship means being there for each other and doing whatever good you can, especially when someone's going through tough times.

More Verses

Romans 12:15 NIV - "Rejoice with those who rejoice; mourn with those who mourn."

Romans 15:13 NIV - "May the God of hope fill you with all joy and peace as you trust in him, so that you may overflow with hope by the power of the Holy Spirit."

How do these verses apply to you? What's the message?

1. **Romans 12:15** is pretty direct, what does it tell you to do with others?

2. According to **Romans 15:13,** what two things will fill you as you trust in God?

Listen Without Fixing

Next time your friend is upset about something, don't try to solve it by suggesting alternatives. Just listen. This will show you care, without needing to fix everything.

Music for Your Heart

Take a moment and listen to
"Gracefully Broken"
by Tasha Cobbs Leonard

Something to Remember

"Encourage everyone you meet with a smile or compliment. Make them feel better when you leave their presence, and they will always be glad to see you coming." - *Joyce Meyer*

Unfair Treatment

1 Peter 3:16 - "Keep a clear conscience, so that those who speak maliciously against your good behavior in Christ may be ashamed of their slander."

Have you ever felt like a teacher was unfairly picking on you, even when you didn't do anything wrong? That's exactly how Jackie felt. Her math teacher seemed to always single her out, blaming her for things she hadn't done. It was frustrating, but losing her cool wasn't what God would want, especially since she was supposed to be an example of Him to the people around her.

One day, after feeling especially upset, Jackie decided she needed to handle this situation differently. Instead of holding on to her frustration, she started praying specifically for her teacher. Every morning before class, Jackie would take a deep breath and ask God to help her stay calm and to give her patience with her teacher. She prayed that God would fill her heart with love, not frustration. It wasn't easy at first, but Jackie noticed a shift in her attitude. Instead of reacting in anger, she found herself staying quiet, choosing to listen instead of arguing.

When you handle unfair treatment with patience and kindness, it shows your strength in Christ. Others notice how you respond and it reflects what it means to follow Jesus. Trusting God during frustrating situations helps you grow in your faith, and your actions could have a bigger impact on those around you than you realize.

More Verses

Matthew 5:44 NIV - "But I tell you, love your enemies and pray for those who persecute you."

James 1:19b NIV - "Everyone should be quick to listen, slow to speak and slow to become angry."

How do these verses apply to you? What's the message?

1. In **Matthew 5:44** what are you to do for people who seem to be against you?

2. How can **James 1:19** help you control your emotions when you're feeling frustrated by unfair treatment?

Pray for the Person

When you're treated unfairly or accused of something you didn't do, ask God to help you see the person through his eyes. Pray for patience, love, and the strength to respond in a way that honors him. Regularly pray for them, especially before seeing the person. It will shift your focus and remind you that God is with you.

Music for Your Heart

Take a moment and listen to
"Battle Belongs"
by Phil Wickham

Something to Remember

"We are to extend forgiveness to others in the same way that God did to us: Unconditionally." - *David Jeremiah*

Community Service

Galatians 5:13 - "You, my brothers and sisters, were called to be free. But do not use your freedom to indulge the flesh; rather, serve one another humbly in love."

Samantha was excited for the weekend. She had plans to hang out with her friends, maybe catch a movie or just relax. But, at youth group, her leader announced a community service project: spending the weekend cleaning up a local park. Samantha wasn't exactly thrilled. It felt like a chore, and she couldn't understand why she had to give up her free time.

Saturday morning, she showed up at the park reluctantly, dragging her feet and hoping it would end quickly. But as she got into the work—picking up trash, planting flowers, and repainting benches—she started noticing something. People walking by would smile, thank the group, and even offer to help. Samantha realized that what she was doing was making a difference. By the end of the day, she felt proud of the work and grateful for the chance to serve.

When you help others with a loving heart, you're not just helping them—you're honoring God. It shifts the focus from yourself and allows you to see the bigger picture: living a life that shows Jesus' love. The joy and purpose you get from serving can totally change how you feel, especially when you see the difference your actions make in someone's life.

More Verses

Mark 10:45 NIV - "For even the Son of Man did not come to be served, but to serve, and to give his life as a ransom for many."

1 Peter 4:10 NIV - "Each of you should use whatever gift you have received to serve others, as faithful stewards of God's grace in its various forms."

How do these verses apply to you? What's the message?

1. How does Jesus' example of serving others in **Mark 10:45** challenge you to serve in your community?

2. In what ways can you use your unique gifts to serve others, as described in **1 Peter 4:10**?

Helping a Neighbor

Help a neighbor by running errands, assisting with yard work, or taking out their trash. You can also offer companionship by spending time with them or helping with technology. Small acts like these can make a big difference in their day.

Music for Your Heart

Take a moment and listen to
"Love God Love People"
by Danny Gokey

Something to Remember

"You can give without loving, but you cannot love without giving."
- *Amy Carmichael*

Love Without Agreeing

Romans 12:18 - "If it is possible, as far as it depends on you, live at peace with everyone."

Sarah sat in the lunchroom listening to a heated conversation about one of her classmates, who had recently come out as transgender. Some of her friends were saying harsh things. Sarah didn't agree with everything, but she knew that responding with unkind words wasn't what Jesus would want. As a Christian, Sarah believed God's word for his design for gender and identity. She also knew that Jesus calls us to love everyone, even when we don't agree with their choices. Sarah asked God for help and decided to speak up with kindness. She wanted to support her friend, stay true to her faith, and show Christ's love without causing drama.

It's not always easy to live out your faith when faced with situations where you don't agree with someone's lifestyle. When you choose to love others, even those you don't agree with, you open the door for God to work in their lives through your example. People are more likely to see Christ through your kindness than through arguments.

More Verses

John 13:34-35 NIV - "A new command I give you: Love one another. As I have loved you, so you must love one another. By this everyone will know that you are my disciples, if you love one another."

Ephesians 4:15 NIV - "Instead, speaking the truth in love, we will grow to become in every respect the mature body of him who is the head, that is, Christ."

How do these verses apply to you? What's the message?

1. In **John 13:34-35**, who gives the command to love one another, who are we called to imitate, and what will others recognize about us if we follow this command?

2. How are we to speak the truth according to **Ephesians 4:15?** How will that affect your life in Christ?

Educate Yourself

Take time to learn how to handle tough conversations where your beliefs differ by reading Christian books, listening to podcasts, or watching videos that teach how to share your faith with love and compassion. You can also talk to trusted youth leaders or pastors to get advice on how to engage respectfully and confidently with others.

Music for Your Heart

Take a moment and listen to
"Jesus, Friend of Sinners"
by Casting Crowns

Something to Remember

"Tolerance isn't about not having beliefs. It's about how your beliefs lead you to treat people who disagree with you." - *Tim Keller*

Boyfriend / Girlfriend

Philippians 1:9-10 - "And this is my prayer: that your love may abound more and more in knowledge and depth of insight, so that you may be able to discern what is best and may be pure and blameless for the day of Christ."

Leah felt the pressure at school when her friends talked about their relationships and how far they had gone with their boyfriends. They often teased her, saying things like, "If you really like Matt, why haven't you taken things further?" Leah knew she wanted to honor God in her relationship, but the constant comments from her friends made it harder to stay strong in her decision. While part of her wanted to fit in, she felt torn because she was committed to staying true to her beliefs and honoring God's plan for her relationship.

What helped Leah stay strong was knowing Matt respected her. He never pressured her to go further physically. Instead, they both agreed to put God first in their relationship, setting clear boundaries that honored God's Word. It wasn't always easy dealing with the pressure from friends, but Leah was glad to be in a relationship where it was built on respect and doing what felt right in God's eyes.

As you grow in your understanding of love, it will help you make choices that honor God. You start to figure out what's best for your relationships and avoid things you might regret later. It keeps the focus on what really matters—respect, staying pure, and treating each other in a way that makes God happy.

More Verses

Philippians 2:5 NIV - "In your relationships with one another, have the same mindset as Christ Jesus."

1 Corinthians 6:19-20 NIV - "Do you not know that your bodies are temples of the Holy Spirit, who is in you, whom you have received from God? You are not your own; you were bought at a price. Therefore, honor God with your bodies."

How do these verses apply to you? What's the message?

1. What attitude or mindset should we have according to **Philippians 2:5?**

2. What does **1 Corinthians 6:19-20** teach about why honoring God with your body is so important?

Unhealthy Influences

Be mindful of the movies, music, and social media you consume. If something pressures you to cross boundaries, choose entertainment that supports your values and helps you honor God and each other. Evaluate your choices, subscriptions, social media and clean them up!

Music for Your Heart

Take a moment and listen to
"Gifts from God"
by Chris Tomlin

Something to Remember

"True love is not about how far you can go, but how much you honor and respect each other." - *Tim Tebow*

Goals, Doodles & Thoughts

Use this space to write or draw about any key points, questions, or goals.

I need you to dream with me.
I need you to believe in a great Lord with me.
I need you to love me in my world.
I need you to walk down the street and reach
out and say,
"Hey brother, may I take your hand and walk
with you?
And you, sister, and you?
May I laugh with you
And cry with you,
And may God and I share
Your lonely roads with you?'
You and God
With love
Can change your world, too.

- Ann Kiemel Anderson

Anxiousness

Philippians 4:6 - "Do not be anxious about anything, but in every situation, by prayer and petition, with thanksgiving, present your requests to God."

Scarlett lay on her bed, staring at the ceiling, her mind racing. It felt like her life was spiraling out of control—arguments at home, pressure from her job, balancing homework, and trying to keep up with everything else. The weight of it all triggered another panic attack, and she could feel the familiar tightness in her chest, her breath getting shorter. But then she noticed the bracelet on her wrist—a simple, leather band with the word "Pray" engraved on it. It was a gift from her best friend, reminding her of the Bible verse they had memorized together: Philippians 4:6.

Scarlett took a deep breath and traced the word with her finger, letting it ground her. Slowly, she whispered the verse aloud: "Do not be anxious about anything..." She closed her eyes and began to pray, just as the verse taught her. It wasn't magic, and her problems didn't disappear instantly, but in that moment, she felt God's peace wash over her. The panic subsided, and for the first time that day, she knew she wasn't alone in her struggles.

When life becomes overwhelming and anxiety hits, God gives us a powerful tool—his word. Even when your problems seem too big to handle, God invites you to bring them to him. Remembering his Word, whether through a bracelet, a note on your phone, or a verse written in your journal, all can be a lifeline during moments of panic. When you focus on God instead of your fears, you invite his peace into your heart and mind.

More Verses

Matthew 6:34 NIV - "Therefore do not worry about tomorrow, for tomorrow will worry about itself. Each day has enough trouble of its own."

Psalm 44:26 NIV - "Rise up and help us; rescue us because of your unfailing love.

How do these verses apply to you? What's the message?

1. What does **Matthew 6:34** say each day has enough of? How should we face tomorrow?

2. In times of trouble, what specific reason does **Psalm 44:26** give for why God will rescue his people?

Physical Reminder

Find a physical reminder, like a bracelet, sticky note, or phone background with a Bible verse that helps you remember to trust God in moments of anxiety.

Music for Your Heart

Take a moment and listen to
"Anxious Heart"
by Jeremy Camp

Something to Remember

"Worry is a cycle of inefficient thoughts whirling around a center of fear."
- *Corrie ten Boom*

Cultural Acceptance

Galatians 3:28 · "There is neither Jew nor Gentile, neither slave nor free, nor is there male and female, for you are all one in Christ Jesus."

Lucia had just moved from Colombia to the U.S., and everything felt different—language, food, even how her classmates dressed. She often sat alone at lunch, feeling out of place as others talked in English using slang she didn't understand. When she spoke in class, her accent made some kids laugh, and it hurt her feelings. She missed the familiar comfort of home.

Rylee, a girl in Lucia's grade, saw her sitting alone and decided to go over and talk with her. She sat with her and started chatting about school and just life. Over the next few weeks, Rylee invited Lucia to hang out with her friends. Rylee prayed every night for Lucia, asking God to help her show kindness and make her feel included.

Rylee knew that being a Christian was the most important part of who she was. It made her see people differently and appreciate them, no matter where they came from. She didn't want anyone to feel left out because of their background. She knew God's family includes people from all over, and he wants us to love each other, no matter our differences.

More Verses

Romans 15:7 NIV · "Accept one another, then, just as Christ accepted you, in order to bring praise to God."

Mark 12:31 NIV · "The second is this: 'Love your neighbor as yourself.' There is no commandment greater than these."

How do these verses apply to you? What's the message?

1. In **Romans 15:7,** how should we accept others according to this verse?

2. In **Mark 12:31,** what does Jesus say we should do for others just like we do for ourselves?

Cultural Opportunity

Reach out to a classmate from a different culture and ask about their favorite tradition, holiday, or food. It's a great way to learn more about them. Commit to pray for them daily for at least one week.

Music for Your Heart

Take a moment and listen to
"All the People Said Amen"
by Matt Maher

Something to Remember

"In Christ, we find our unity and our identity, no matter where we're from."
- *Priscilla Shirer*

Busy Parents

2 Corinthians 6:18 - "I will be a Father to you, and you will be my sons and daughters, says the Lord Almighty."

Jenna always thought parents were supposed to be there to help their kids navigate life-teaching them how to handle challenges and grow into who they're meant to be. But lately, she felt like her parents didn't see what she needed. When her mom missed another one of her events or her dad rushed off to work without checking in, she couldn't help but feel let down. "Shouldn't they be the ones showing me how to handle life and be there for me?" she wondered.

One Saturday, sitting alone at the breakfast table again, Jenna remembered a church lesson about God always being there for us, even when others aren't. "God is our Father too," the youth pastor had said. That stuck with her. She grabbed a sticky note and wrote, "Hope you have a great day! Love you!" and stuck it on the fridge. It was small, but it was her way of choosing love over frustration.

Jenna realized that while her parents might be busy, God could fill the spaces they couldn't. She was learning to rely on God as her guide and comforter, no longer expecting her parents to meet every need. In return, God gave her the strength to love them, even when they were too busy.

More Verses

Deuteronomy 31:8 NIV - "The Lord himself goes before you and will be with you; He will never leave you nor forsake you. Do not be afraid; do not be discouraged."

Psalm 68:5 NIV - "A father to the fatherless, a defender of widows, is God in His holy dwelling."

How do these verses apply to you? What's the message?

1. How awesome is it to know that God goes before you...each and every day! What will he never do according to **Deuteronomy 31:8?** What does he tell you not to be as a result?

2. In **Psalm 68:5,** who is God a father to?

Parental Love

Leave a quick note for your parents like, "Hope you have an awesome day!" or make their coffee or tea to give them a little boost. Say a quick prayer for them, asking God to watch over them. Send a quick text like, "Thinking about you! Hope your day's going great!" to show you're thinking of them.

Music for Your Heart
Take a moment and listen to
"Good Good Father"
by Chris Tomlin

Something to Remember

"Trust involves letting go and knowing God will catch you." - *James Dobson*

Serving Others

Acts 20:35 - " In everything I did, I showed you that by this kind of hard work we must help the weak, remembering the words the Lord Jesus himself said: 'It is more blessed to give than to receive."

When Harper signed up for a mission trip to Honduras, she had no idea what to expect. She'd heard stories, but it wasn't until she was there, helping build a school, that it hit her. The kids were super excited to see the school come together, but what really got to Harper was how grateful they were for stuff she always took for granted—clean water, food, even basic classrooms.

As the week went on, Harper realized how different life was there compared to back home. She was so used to having everything she needed, and seeing how much they appreciated what they had was humbling. It made her think about how often she complained about little things that didn't really matter. Serving in Honduras opened her eyes to how blessed she was, and she realized God was calling her to not just help others but to be more thankful for everything she had.

Helping people who don't have much totally changes how you see things. It makes you stop thinking about your own problems and realize how much you've actually been given.

More Verses

Matthew 20:28 NIV - "Just as the Son of Man did not come to be served, but to serve, and to give his life as a ransom for many."

Proverbs 22:4 NIV - "Humility is the fear of the Lord; its wages are riches and honor and life."

How do these verses apply to you? What's the message?

1. **Matthew 20:28** what did the Son of Man come to do? What was his greatest act of service?

2. According to **Proverbs 22:4,** what are the rewards of humility and fear of the Lord?

Money Abroad

Create a fundraiser for a mission organization your church supports. Get your youth group, friends, and even adults to pitch in for a month. At the end, see how much you all raised, and send it to the mission with a note saying you're praying for them and their work.

Music for Your Heart

Take a moment and listen to
"Give Me Your Eyes"
by Brandon Heath

Something to Remember

"There is no improving the future without disturbing the present."
- *Catherine Booth*

Self-Control

Proverbs 25:28 - "Like a city whose walls are broken through is a person who lacks self-control."

Lily felt like her life was spinning out of control. Her emotions were all over the place—angry at her sister for borrowing her shirt one minute, overwhelmed by anxiety about exams the next. Her friends wanted her to stay out late on school nights when she had homework, and she often snapped at her mom or sent texts she regretted. It felt like her emotions were running her life, and it was exhausting.

One night, Lily decided to spend some time with God and came across Proverbs 25:28. She realized that she was like that city without walls, letting every feeling and pressure from the outside world dictate her actions. That night, she prayed, asking God for forgiveness and help. It would take time, so she started small. She learned to say "no" when pressured by friends, put her phone down when overwhelmed, and paused before speaking when frustrated. Each step was progress, plus she was relying on God!

Being a teenager can feel overwhelming, with emotions all over the place, and it can be hard to stay focused. Without self-control, it's easy to let those emotions take charge, like a city with no walls to protect it. God's word reminds us to build strong "walls" of self-control, so we don't get caught up in temptations.

More Verses

Galatians 5:22-23 NIV - "But the fruit of the Spirit is love, joy, peace, forbearance, kindness, goodness, faithfulness, gentleness and self-control."

Ephesians 6:12 NIV - "For our struggle is not against flesh and blood, but against the rulers, against the authorities, against the powers of this dark world and against the spiritual forces of evil in the heavenly realms."

How do these verses apply to you? What's the message?

1. From **Galatians 5:22-23,** what actions do you find hardest to control? Ask the Holy Spirit to help you.

2. In **Ephesians 6:12,** who does it say our struggle is not against, and who is it really against?

Self-Control Practice

For one week, pick something to work on, like limiting your screen time to one hour or pausing before reacting when you're upset. Each day, write down how you did in a journal—what went well and what was hard. Ask God for help each day, and at the end of the week, look back and see how much you've improved!

Music for Your Heart

Take a moment and listen to
"Control"
by Tenth Avenue North

Something to Remember

"When God calls you to do something, he's not calling you because you're ready. He's calling you because he is ready." - *Bianca Olthoff*

Goals, Doodles & Thoughts

Use this space to write or draw about any key points, questions, or goals.

Isaiah 65:24 NKJV

It shall come to pass that before they call, I will answer; And while they are still speaking, I will hear.

This verse provides us with an incredible picture of our Lord's love for us. Evidently, he is so anxious to bless us, so ready to fulfill his loving-kindness in our lives, that he can't even wait for us to tell him our needs. So, he jumps in and performs acts of mercy, grace and love toward us. That is a supreme pleasure to him.

- David Wilkerson

Hope in Darkness

Psalm 34:18 - "The Lord is close to the brokenhearted and saves those who are crushed in spirit."

Audrey scrolled through Instagram again, feeling worse with every post. Everyone seemed prettier, happier, and more popular than her. Her grades were dropping, her best friend wasn't speaking to her, and her parents kept fighting about money. She felt stuck and just wanted to stay in bed, shutting everyone out.

At school, she felt invisible, like no one would notice if she disappeared. She had never felt this low before and didn't know how to make it stop.

That night, sitting alone in the dark, Audrey remembered a Bible study from months ago. She couldn't recall everything, but a verse about God being close to the brokenhearted stood out. Desperate, she searched for it and found Psalm 34:18: "The Lord is close to the brokenhearted and saves those who are crushed in spirit."

She whispered a small prayer, asking God to be with her. For the first time in a while, she felt a tiny bit of hope. Maybe God really was closer than she thought.

Just like Audrey, when we feel low, God's word reminds us he's with us, even in our hardest moments. Psalm 34:18 shows us that while the pain might not disappear right away, God's presence gives us strength and hope.

More Verses

Isaiah 40:31 NIV - "But those who hope in the Lord will renew their strength. They will soar on wings like eagles; they will run and not grow weary, they will walk and not be faint."

Matthew 11:28 NIV - "Come to me, all you who are weary and burdened, and I will give you rest."

How do these verses apply to you? What's the message?

1. **According to Isaiah 40:31** what happens to those who hope in the Lord?

2. When you need rest from feeling overwhelmed, what does **Matthew 11:28** say to do?

Scripture In Your Face

Write out Psalm 34:18 and keep it somewhere you can see it every day, like a mirror or notebook. Make sure to post it a few places so you see it all day long...it is his promise to you.

Music for Your Heart

Take a moment and listen to
"Known"
by Tauren Wells

Something to Remember

"There is no pit so deep that God's love is not deeper still." - *Corrie ten Boom*

Gods' Word is Truth

John 17:17 · "Sanctify them by the truth; your word is truth."

Maria sat on her bed, overwhelmed by social media arguments about religion and posts about innocent people suffering. Her friend Natalia texted, "How can you believe in a loving God when good people are getting hurt?" Feeling confused, Maria called her youth leader.

She shared her thoughts and asked the big question, "How do I know that the God of the Bible is the truth?" Her leader reminded her that while the world is filled with different opinions, God's Word is clear. He pointed her to John 17:17—God's Word is truth. He explained that even though we may not always understand why things happen the way they do, we can trust that God's character never changes. The pain and suffering in the world are real, but so is the truth that God loves us and has a bigger plan beyond what we can see right now.

When you focus on God's word, the confusion around you starts to fade. Even though people have different opinions about life, religion, and even God, the Bible is always a reliable source of truth. Understanding what God says helps you stay confident in your faith, even when others question it. And while it's tough to understand why bad things happen, the Bible reminds us of God's love, his plan, and that he will always be fair, even when we don't fully get it.

More Verses

Psalm 119:160 NIV - "All your words are true; all your righteous laws are eternal."

Proverbs 30:5 NIV - "Every word of God is flawless; he is a shield to those who take refuge in him."

How do these verses apply to you? What's the message?

1. What two things does **Psalm 119:160** tells us about God's Word?

2. In **Proverbs 30:5,** what do we know about the word of God? How does it protect us?

Ready with an Answer

When you encounter something that makes you question God's truth—whether in a conversation, social media, or class—write down your question. Then, look for answers in the Bible, ask a trusted Christian mentor or teacher, and pray for understanding.

Music for Your Heart

Take a moment and listen to
"I Believe It"
by Jon Reddick

Something to Remember

"The truth of God's Word is not subject to the opinions of people. It stands firm through every challenge, every doubt, and every storm." - *Elisabeth Elliot*

The Power of Truth

John 8:32 - "Then you will know the truth, and the truth will set you free."

Natalia sat on the bleachers at school, her phone glowing with messages. She had been hanging out with a new group of girls, and at first, it seemed like they were fun. But lately, Natalia noticed how they would gossip about others and twist the truth to fit their own stories. Today, one of the girls had started a rumor about her, claiming she had said something hurtful about another classmate. As she read the messages from her friends, she felt trapped in a lie she hadn't even told. She didn't know what to do. Should she confront them? Ignore it?

Later that night, while scrolling through music, Natalia stumbled upon the song, *The Truth* by Megan Woods. The lyrics hit home: she realized how freeing it would be to stop avoiding the truth and speak up about what was really happening.

When you live in God's truth, you don't have to carry the weight of lies or fear anymore. Being real with yourself and others because of God's truth makes you feel more confident, at peace, and clear about who you are. Even when people try to tear you down, God's truth never changes. Choosing to speak and live out his truth can help you build better friendships, stay strong inside, and stand your ground when life gets tough.

More Verses

Ephesians 4:25 NIV - "Therefore each of you must put off falsehood and speak truthfully to your neighbor, for we are all members of one body."

Proverbs 12:22 NIV - "The Lord detests lying lips, but he delights in people who are trustworthy."

How do these verses apply to you? What's the message?

1. In **Ephesians 4:25,** what are you to stop doing and what are you to start doing? Why?

2. Who does God delight in according to **Proverbs 12:22,** and what does he detest?

Telling the Truth

If you've said something that wasn't true, think about going back to that person and being real with them. Even just saying, "Hey, I need to be honest with you," could totally change how things turn out.

Music for Your Heart

Take a moment and listen to
"The Truth"
by Megan Woods

Something to Remember

"Honesty and transparency make you vulnerable. Be honest and transparent anyway." - *Mother Teresa*

Impossible Situations

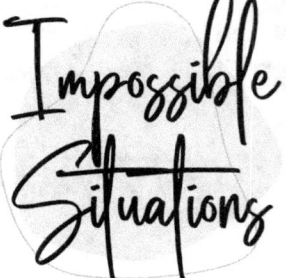

Mark 10:27 - "Jesus looked at them and said, 'With man this is impossible, but not with God; all things are possible with God."

Lily's world had been completely shaken. Just weeks before college application deadlines, her mom was diagnosed with stage 4 cancer. Now, as Lily sat in the hospital room beside her mom's bed, her phone buzzed with an email. She opened it and froze. Her application to Stanford, the school she'd dreamed of for years, had been deferred—she'd have to wait even longer for a decision. Swallowing her disappointment, she shared the news with her mom. To Lily's surprise, her mom's eyes sparkled with determination. "Then show them why they should pick you," her mom said firmly, her voice steady despite her frail condition.

Overwhelmed, Lily asked, "But what if you need me here?" Her mom squeezed her hand. "What I need is for you to live your life. Remember, with God, all things are possible."

Lily had to trust God, even when everything looked hopeless. She looked at her frail mother and thought about her uncertain college prospects, it all seemed impossible. Maybe God didn't want her to go to college right now. Maybe this was a sign she should stay home. Or maybe this was a test of her faith. She started praying not just for her mom's healing and her college admission, but for God's will to be done and for the strength to face whatever came next.

Believing God can do anything gives us hope when life gets crazy. It doesn't mean everything will be perfect, but it reminds us God's working behind the scenes. Even when life's confusing or scary, we can find peace knowing God's got a plan.

More Verses

Jeremiah 32:27 NIV - "I am the Lord, the God of all mankind. Is anything too hard for me?"

Matthew 19:26 NIV - "Jesus looked at them and said, 'With man this is impossible, but with God all things are possible."

How do these verses apply to you? What's the message?

1. **Jeremiah 32:27** tells us what about the ability of God?

2. What is possible when we put our faith and trust in God according to **Matthew 19:26 & Mark 10:27?** ☺

Prayer Board

Create a prayer board in your room. Write down your concerns, hopes, and prayers, and update it regularly as a visual reminder of God's work in your life. You will see his answers and directions as you trust! Be excited!

Music for Your Heart

Take a moment and listen to
"Giants Fall"
by Francesca Battistelli

Something to Remember

"Faith is not about everything turning out OK; faith is about being OK no matter how things turn out." - *Lisa Bevere*

Humble Confidence

Colossians 3:23 · "Whatever you do, work at it with all your heart, as working for the Lord, not for human masters."

Hannah had always loved singing, and this year she was thrilled to perform her first solo at the school concert. She had worked hard and was grateful for the chance to use the talent God had given her. Over the months, she and her best friend, Audrey, had sung at local nursing homes, some local events, and even some restaurants. They always hoped to brighten people's day.

As the concert got closer, Hannah couldn't believe how much her love for singing had grown. With colleges starting to notice her performances, she felt more motivated than ever to keep practicing and get better. She wanted to nail it and make everyone proud. When she walked out for her solo, instead of feeling nervous, she felt this rush of excitement. This was her moment, and she was ready to own it. As the audience clapped, Hannah grinned, knowing all her hard work had paid off. She felt lucky to have a talent she could share with others; and grateful to God for allowing her to sing!

God gives each of us talents, and he wants us to enjoy and use them to serve others and honor him. Your gifts aren't just for success or attention—they're for a greater purpose. Whether it's writing, baking, photography, or anything else, trust that God's strength helps you do great things with what he's blessed you with.

More Verses

1 Corinthians 10:31 NIV · "So whether you eat or drink or whatever you do, do it all for the glory of God."

I Corinthians 15:58 NIV · "Therefore, my dear brothers and sisters, stand firm. Let nothing move you. Always give yourselves fully to the work of the Lord, because you know that your labor in the Lord is not in vain."

How do these verses apply to you? What's the message?

1. In **1 Corinthians 10:31,** what does it say we should do for the glory of God?

2. According to **1 Corinthians 15:58,** how should we stand in our faith, and why should we give ourselves fully to the work of the Lord?

Sharing Your Talent

Find someone younger than you who shares your talent, like singing or drawing, and offer to share some tips to help them improve. Work together, cheer each other on, and find fun ways to use your gifts to make a difference for God.

Music for Your Heart

Take a moment and listen to
"Dream Small"
by Josh Wilson

Something to Remember

"Humility is not thinking less of yourself but thinking of yourself less."
- *C.S. Lewis*

Goals, Doodles & Thoughts

Use this space to write or draw about any key points, questions, or goals.

Not forgiving is like drinking poison and hoping another person will die.

- Voice of Martyrs, 2017

Procrastination

Ecclesiastes 11:4 - "Whoever watches the wind will not plant; whoever looks at the clouds will not reap."

Georgia had a bad habit of putting things off. Her room was always a mess; despite promising herself she'd clean it days ago. She also forgot to make a reservation for her mom's birthday dinner, and now her mom was disappointed. On top of that, her younger brother needed help with a project, but Georgia kept delaying it. Then came her homework—a big project due tomorrow. Instead of starting early, she wasted hours scrolling through social media. Now, with the deadline looming, she felt overwhelmed. Georgia realized that procrastination was not only creating stress but making her feel like she wasn't living up to her potential or God's calling.

It wasn't easy, but Georgia decided to start tackling her list one thing at a time. She prayed for God's help and energy, then began with the homework project. Once it was finished, she felt a small spark of relief—and even a little pride. That feeling motivated her to tackle her messy room. Slowly but surely, things started falling into place.

When we do what God says about not being lazy, we actually feel better and less stressed because we get things done on time. It feels great to finish something and know we gave it our best. Plus, it shows God that we're serious about using our time wisely.

More Verses

Ephesians 5:15-16 NIV - ""Be very careful, then, how you live—not as unwise but as wise, making the most of every opportunity, because the days are evil."

Colossians 3:23 NIV - "Whatever you do, work at it with all your heart, as working for the Lord, not for human masters."

How do these verses apply to you? What's the message?

1. According to **Ephesians 5:15-16,** how are you to live? What are you to do with opportunity?

2. How does **Colossians 3:23** tell us to do our work and who do we work for?

Set the Timer

Make a simple to-do list and put the hardest thing at the top so you can get it out of the way first. Then, set a timer for 20 minutes and focus on doing just that one thing without any distractions. You'll be surprised how much you can get done!

Music for Your Heart

Take a moment and listen to
"Jesus Does"
by We the Kingdom

Something to Remember

"When we avoid work, we cheat ourselves and others of the blessings God wants to give." - *Charles Stanley*

Talk to Jesus

Jeremiah 33:2-3 · "This is what the Lord says, he who made the earth, the Lord who formed it and established it—the Lord is his name: 'Call to me and I will answer you and tell you great and unsearchable things you do not know."

Samantha nervously fidgeted with her bracelet as she sat in the circle at youth group. Her heart raced when the leader asked if anyone wanted to close in prayer. She'd always admired how easily some of her friends could pray out loud, their words flowing effortlessly. But for Samantha, the thought of praying in front of others made her palms sweat. What if she said something wrong? What if her words didn't sound "holy" enough?

As the silence stretched on, Samantha took a deep breath and whispered, "God, help me." To her surprise, she felt a sense of calm wash over her. She realized that prayer wasn't about impressing others or using fancy words. It was simply about talking to Jesus, her friend who knew her heart. With newfound courage, Samantha raised her hand and offered to pray.

When we understand that prayer is just talking to Jesus, it takes away the pressure to perform. We can approach God with honesty and openness, sharing our thoughts, fears, and dreams without fear of judgment. This open communication strengthens our relationship with God and encourages others to step out of their comfort zones as well.

More Verses

Jeremiah 29:12-13 NIV - "Then you will call on me and come and pray to me, and I will listen to you. You will seek me and find me when you seek me with all your heart."

Romans 8:26 NIV - "In the same way, the Spirit helps us in our weakness. We do not know what we ought to pray for, but the Spirit himself intercedes for us through wordless groans."

How do these verses apply to you? What's the message?

1. In **Jeremiah 29:12-13,** what does God promise when you pray, and how should you seek Him to find Him?

2. According to **Romans 8:26,** who helps you pray when you don't know what to say to the Lord?

Prayer Challenges

This week, set a timer for 2 minutes to talk to Jesus about your day, like He's right next to you, and then offer to pray with a close friend or family member.

Music for Your Heart

Take a moment and listen to
"Praise You Anywhere"
by Brandon Lake

Something to Remember

"Prayer is simply talking to God like a friend and should be the easiest thing we do each day." - *Joyce Meyer*

Evangelism Road Trip

Matthew 28:19 · "Therefore go and make disciples of all nations, baptizing them in the name of the Father and of the Son and of the Holy Spirit."

Kelsey and her friends had been talking for weeks about going on a mini road trip together. It wasn't far, just a few towns over, but they were excited to get out, explore, and enjoy some freedom. As they were planning, Kelsey felt a nudge in her heart. What if this trip wasn't just about fun? What if they made it an opportunity to share Jesus with people they met along the way?

At first, she was nervous. What if they got weird looks? What if people rejected them? But she remembered her youth group lesson on sharing her faith with others. Jesus didn't ask them to be perfect or worry about how people would respond—he simply asked them to go and share his love. So, with a few Bibles in their backpacks and hearts full of hope, Kelsey and her friends hit the road, ready to share Jesus wherever they stopped.

When you take a step of faith and talk about Jesus with others, even in small ways, it boosts your confidence in what you believe and reminds you of how much God loves everyone. By focusing on others and sharing his love, you'll not only grow closer to God but also show people who might be struggling that there's real hope and love available to them!

More Verses

Mark 16:15 NIV - "He said to them, 'Go into all the world and preach the gospel to all creation.'"

Romans 10:14 NIV - "How, then, can they call on the one they have not believed in? And how can they believe in the one of whom they have not heard? And how can they hear without someone preaching to them?"

How do these verses apply to you? What's the message?

1. **Mark 16:15** challenges us to go out and do what?

2. In reading **Romans 10:14** it reminds us that people need us to do what in order for them to hear about God?

Sharing Jesus

Think of three clever ways to share Jesus at your next get-together with friends. You could brighten someone's day by leaving an encouraging note with a Bible verse for a stranger or surprise a friend with a thoughtful gift that shares a Christian message. Get creative and make it meaningful!

Music for Your Heart

Take a moment and listen to
"The Commission"
by Cain

Something to Remember

"You may never know how even a small word about Jesus can impact someone's life forever." - *Beth Moore*

Share a Devotional

Proverbs 27:17 - "As iron sharpens iron, so one person sharpens another."

Lainey and her friends had a new tradition. Every Friday after school, they'd meet up at their favorite coffee shop, but instead of just chatting about the latest drama or their weekend plans, they started sharing their devotionals. Each girl brought something different—sometimes it was a Bible verse that had really spoken to them, other times it was a story from a Christian book they were reading.

At first, Lainey was nervous. What if her friends didn't connect with the devotional she shared? But after hearing her friend Alice talk about how God was helping her be more patient, Lainey realized then that their sharing didn't have to be super deep or perfectly polished—just honest. They were all in this together—growing and learning from each other's experiences with God. By sharing, they were helping each other grow stronger in their faith, just like Proverbs 27:17 says. They were "sharpening" each other, encouraging each other, and learning more about God's love every time they met.

When you talk about what God is doing in your life, you not only encourage your friends, but you also start to see more clearly how God is working in your own heart. Hearing how God is speaking to others reminds you that you're not alone in your struggles and victories. It builds a supportive group where everyone can grow together in faith.

More Verses

Proverbs 12:26a NIV - The righteous choose their friends carefully.

Ephesians 4:16 NIV - "From him the whole body, joined and held together by every supporting ligament, grows and builds itself up in love, as each part does its work."

How do these verses apply to you? What's the message?

1. What does **Proverbs 12:26a** say about how the righteous choose their friendships?

2. According to **Ephesians 4:16,** how does the body of Christ grow and build itself up?

Devotional Swap

Write out a short journal entry about what God is doing in your life and send it to a friend. From that, try to organize a "devotional swap" with your friends. Each person can bring their favorite verse or story to share and discuss. This way, you'll encourage each other and build a close group that grows stronger in their understanding of the Word of God.

Music for Your Heart

Take a moment and listen to
"This Could Change Everything"
by Francesca Battistelli

Something to Remember

"In community, we find strength to follow Jesus boldly."
- *Sadie Robertson Huff*

Helping Out

Matthew 7:12 · "So in everything, do to others what you would have them do to you, for this sums up the Law and the Prophets."

Anna was running late for her history class. She had stayed up too late watching videos and now barely had enough time to get to school, let alone grab a good seat. As she rushed down the hall, she saw a girl named Cora trip and spill her books everywhere. Anna didn't really know Cora, and to be honest, she was tempted to walk right by. After all, she didn't want to be late. But as Anna saw Cora scrambling to pick up her papers with her face turning red, she remembered a time when she had dropped her own books and wished someone had helped. Even though it would make her a few minutes late, Anna decided to stop and help.

How we treat others matters to God, even when it's uncomfortable or inconvenient. God calls us to love and serve others as we would want to be loved. Anna's small decision to help Cora was showing kindness in a simple moment. When we step out of our comfort zones to help others, we not only lift their burdens but reflect Christ's love. These small acts can brighten someone's day, strengthen our own character, and may even lead to new friendships. Plus, you'll feel good knowing you made a difference.

More Verses

Hebrews 13:16 NIV - "And do not forget to do good and to share with others, for with such sacrifices God is pleased."

I Timothy 6:18 NIV - "Command them to do good, to be rich in good deeds, and to be generous and willing to share."

How do these verses apply to you? What's the message?

1. In **Hebrews 13:16,** what two things are we encouraged to do, and why are they important?

2. What does **1 Timothy 6:18** say about how we should act toward others?

Opportunities

Start a habit of praying each morning for God to open your eyes to someone who needs help or encouragement each day. Spend a few minutes asking God to show you someone who may need support, whether it's someone who looks lonely, a friend having a rough time, or someone who just needs help. Then, act on what God shows you—offer encouragement, lend a hand, or simply listen.

Music for Your Heart

Take a moment and listen to
"Brother"
by NEEDTOBREATHE (featuring
Gavin DeGraw)

Something to Remember

"Do all the good you can, by all the means you can, in all the ways you can, in all the places you can, at all the times you can, to all the people you can, as long as ever you can." - *John Wesley*

Goals, Doodles & Thoughts

Use this space to write or draw about any key points, questions, or goals.

The journey into risk is a venture into faith.

- *Chuck Swindoll*

Giving with Joy

2 Corinthians 9:7 - "Each of you should give what you have decided in your heart to give, not reluctantly or under compulsion, for God loves a cheerful giver."

Olivia stared at her phone, scrolling through the latest posts on Instagram. Her best friend, Mia, had just shared pictures from her mission trip to Guatemala. Olivia felt a twinge of envy mixed with admiration. She had wanted to go on that trip too, but the cost seemed out of reach. As she continued scrolling, an ad for the newest iPhone caught her eye. She had been saving up for months, and now she finally had enough. But something made her pause. Was this really the best use of her money?

God's word reminds us that giving shouldn't be a chore or something we do out of guilt. Instead, it should come from a place of joy and willingness. When we give cheerfully, we're not just helping others – we're also positioning our hearts with God's generous nature. When we choose to give with a happy heart, we get to experience the real excitement and meaning that comes from being generous.

More Verses

Proverbs 11:24-25 NIV - "One person gives freely, yet gains even more; another withholds unduly, but comes to poverty. A generous person will prosper; whoever refreshes others will be refreshed."

Luke 6:38 NIV - "Give, and it will be given to you. A good measure, pressed down, shaken together and running over, will be poured into your lap. For with the measure you use, it will be measured to you."

How do these verses apply to you? What's the message?

1. According to **Proverbs 11:24-25,** what results can we expect for someone who gives freely, is generous, and refreshes others?

2. According to **Luke 6:38,** how does Jesus say God will give back to us? Can you spot the four ways he describes it?

Money to Give

Set aside a portion of your money for giving. Start with 10% of your allowance or paycheck. Instead of buying that new outfit or gadget you've been eyeing, consider donating that money to your church's youth mission fund, a cause you care about or the church you attend.

Music for Your Heart

Take a moment and listen to
"Only Jesus"
by Casting Crowns

Something to Remember

"When you give to God, you discover that God gives to you." - *Rick Warren*

No to Temptation

1 Corinthians 10:13 · "No temptation has overtaken you except what is common to mankind. And God is faithful; he will not let you be tempted beyond what you can bear. But when you are tempted, he will also provide a way out so that you can endure it."

Kayla had recently become a Christian and was starting to see changes in her life—better friends, healthier habits, and more peace in her heart. But one weekend, an old friend texted her, asking her to come to a party. Kayla knew this wasn't just any party—she had been to parties like this before where drugs were passed around, and it was easy to get caught up in the moment. Part of her missed the excitement of that lifestyle, and the idea of fitting in again with her old friends was tempting. She even thought, "Maybe just this once wouldn't hurt."

But deep down, Kayla remembered how lost and empty she felt before she gave her life to Christ. After a few moments of struggling with the urge to go back to her old ways, she decided to text one of her new friends and they made plans to hang out. Even though it wasn't easy, Kayla managed to say no, trusting that God would help her through. She just had to make the choice!

We all face temptations that pull us back toward things we know aren't good for us, especially after we've started walking with Christ. It's easy to be tempted by old habits, but God promises to help us resist. When you say no, you're protecting the stronger, new version of yourself that God's creating. Each time you resist, you're getting more confident and closer to the better life God has for you. And over time, those old temptations won't have the same pull on you anymore.

More Verses

James 1:14 NIV · "But each person is tempted when they are dragged away by their own evil desire and enticed."

Hebrews 2:18 NIV · "Because he himself suffered when he was tempted, he is able to help those who are being tempted."

How do these verses apply to you? What's the message?

1. In **James 1:14,** what does it say leads people into temptation?

2. According to **Hebrews 2:18,** why is Jesus able to help those who are being tempted?

Temptation ToolKit

Put together a "Temptation Toolkit" with a small box filled with Bible verses, prayers, gratitude notes, and positive quotes. Add a journal to write about your struggles and wins, and maybe include a few pictures or keepsakes that remind you of your life with Christ. Use it whenever you're feeling tempted to help you stay focused on God's promises and make choices you can feel good about.

Music for Your Heart

Take a moment and listen to
"The Father's House"
by Cory Asbury

Something to Remember

"God's strength is the perfect weapon against temptation. We don't have to fight it alone." - *Lysa TerKeurst*

You are Important

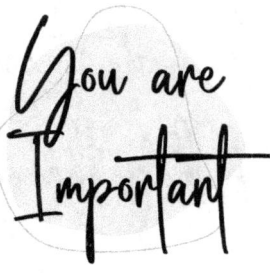

Romans 8:38-39 · "For I am convinced that neither death nor life, neither angels nor demons, neither the present nor the future, nor any powers, neither height nor depth, nor anything else in all creation, will be able to separate us from the love of God that is in Christ Jesus our Lord."

Sydney stared out her bedroom window, her headphones blasting music in an attempt to drown out her thoughts. School had been brutal—again. Her so-called friends had ignored her all week, and the cruel messages they'd sent still replayed in her mind. At home, things weren't much better. Her parents were always arguing, and Sydney felt like she didn't matter to anyone.

The ache in her chest felt heavier than ever as she pulled her knees to her chest, fighting back tears. The thought hit her hard and fast: "Maybe it would be better if I wasn't here." It scared her how much she believed it in that moment.

In the midst of her pain, Sydney's phone buzzed. It was a simple message from her youth leader: "Hey, thinking about you today. God loves you so much—don't forget that." Sydney stared at the message, and for the first time all day, she let the tears fall.

That night, she picked up her Bible, searching for something to hold on to. The words she read hit her deeply—nothing could separate her from God's love. Not her sadness, mistakes, or doubts. His love was steady, unbreakable, and real, no matter how she felt.

When you're feeling broken or like no one cares, remember this: God's love isn't based on how you feel or what you're going through. His love is bigger than anything you're facing—even the darkest thoughts. Nothing you've done, no mistake, no situation, can make him stop loving you. **You matter, and you're not alone.**

More Verses

Psalm 55:22 NIV - "Cast your cares on the Lord and he will sustain you; he will never let the righteous be shaken."

John 16:33 NIV - "I have told you these things, so that in me you may have peace. In this world you will have trouble. But take heart! I have overcome the world."

How do these verses apply to you? What's the message?

1. In **Psalm 55:22,** what should we do with our burdens, and what does God promise in return?

2. According to **John 16:33,** this world brings trouble. But what do we receive from God, and what has He done to the world?

Creative Goals List

Take a notebook or colorful paper and write two types of goals: short-term and long-term. List them out – make yourself see a future and make it a good one! Get creative! Use markers, colored pencils, or stickers to decorate around your goals. Add Bible verses, such as Proverbs 3:5-6 or Jeremiah 29:11, to remind you that God is guiding your future.

Music for Your Heart

Take a moment and listen to
"Surrounded"
by Michael W. Smith

Something to Remember

"You don't have to fight for a place at the table when you realize God has already prepared one for you." - *Lisa Bevere*

Little Stuff

Proverbs 3:5 - "Trust in the Lord with all your heart and lean not on your own understanding."

Summer slumped onto her bed, her head spinning. The day had been a disaster. She'd spilled coffee on her favorite hoodie that morning, completely bombed her math quiz, and forgotten to bring the poster she was supposed to present in history. If that wasn't bad enough, her group chat exploded with drama that afternoon, and now her mom was upset because Summer hadn't cleaned her room—again.

It wasn't just one thing; it was everything. Each little mistake piled up until it felt like she couldn't breathe. Summer grabbed her pillow and screamed into it. Why did it feel like she was failing at life?

Later that night, as she scrolled aimlessly on her phone, she glanced up and noticed a sticky note on her mirror. It was a reminder her dad had given her months ago: Trust God, even when life feels impossible. Summer stared at it. She hadn't thought about trusting God much lately. She'd been so focused on trying to fix everything herself that she hadn't even prayed.

With a deep sigh, Summer decided to try. She whispered a simple prayer: God, I feel like I can't handle all of this. Help me trust you.

When life feels like it's falling apart, you don't have to fix everything by yourself. Trusting God means letting him guide you through the mess. He cares about even the smallest details of your life and will give you strength to handle what's in front of you. Take a deep breath, say a prayer, and let him take the lead.

More Verses

Jeremiah 17:7-8 NIV - "But blessed is the one who trusts in the Lord, whose confidence is in him; they will be like a tree planted by the water that sends out its roots by the stream. It does not fear when heat comes; its leaves are always green, it has no worries in a year of drought, and it never fails to bear fruit."

Psalm 28:7 NIV - "The Lord is my strength and my shield; my heart trusts in him, and he helps me. My heart leaps for joy, and with my song I praise him."

How do these verses apply to you? What's the message?

1. In **Jeremiah 17:7-8,** what are the blessings for the person who trusts in the Lord, and how are they compared to a tree planted by water?

2. In **Psalm 28:7,** how does David describe the Lord's role in his life, and how does he respond because of it?

10 Second Breathing

Next time something small goes wrong, like forgetting your homework or losing your keys, pause for 10 seconds. Take a deep breath and ask Jesus to help you stay calm. Imagine him helping you think clearly as you handle the situation. Then, smile and choose to approach it with patience, trusting that he's guiding you through even the small frustrations.

Music for Your Heart

Take a moment and listen to
"This is the Stuff"
by Francesca Battistelli

Something to Remember

"If we throw up our hands and give up when things feel hard, we will never experience the miracles God has for us on the other side of that hard."
- *Jennie Allen*

Exceptional Wisdom

1 Kings 4:29 - "God gave Solomon wisdom and very great insight, and a breadth of understanding as measureless as the sand on the seashore."

Isabel sat on her bed, scrolling through her phone. Her friend had just asked for advice about a situation that was really tough, and Isabel wasn't sure how to respond. She wanted to help, but she didn't feel like she had the wisdom for it. Taking a deep breath, Isabel closed her eyes and remembered one of the verses she had memorized: "If any of you lacks wisdom, ask God, and he will give it to you generously." She whispered a prayer, asking God for wisdom to speak the right words.

Later that day, when her friend called again, Isabel felt a calm sense of knowing better what to say. She shared advice that surprised even her—it felt like God had given her just the right words. Isabel smiled as she hung up, realizing that God truly listens and answers prayers for wisdom.

When you ask God for wisdom, you're inviting him to help you in every part of your life, not just to solve problems but to give you peace and clarity. His wisdom helps you see things in a new way, and as you trust him, he'll guide you through decisions and moments that feel confusing. With God's help, you can move forward with confidence, knowing he's leading you every step of the way.

More Verses

James 1:5 NIV - "If any of you lacks wisdom, you should ask God, who gives generously to all without finding fault, and it will be given to you."

Proverbs 2:6 NIV - "For the Lord gives wisdom; from his mouth come knowledge and understanding."

How do these verses apply to you? What's the message?

1. After reading **James 1:5,** what will God give you just by asking him?

2. What does **Proverbs 2:6** say is the source of wisdom, knowledge, and understanding?

Ask God, He Knows Stuff

Take a few minutes today to pray and ask God for wisdom in one area of your life where you're feeling unsure. Write down three Bible verses that talk about wisdom and think about them this the week. The next time you're stuck, take a moment to pause and ask God to guide your decisions.

Music for Your Heart

Take a moment and listen to
"Honestly We Just Need Jesus"
by Terrian

Something to Remember

"True wisdom is a divine gift, a result of seeking God earnestly in prayer."
- Elisabeth Elliot

Goals, Doodles & Thoughts

Use this space to write or draw about any key points, questions, or goals.

Deliberately tell God that you will not fret about whatever concerns you. All our fretting and worrying is caused by planning without God.

- Oswald Chambers

Philippians 4:6-7 AMP – Classic Edition

Do not be anxious or worried about anything, but in everything [every circumstance and situation] by prayer and petition with thanksgiving, continue to make your [specific] requests known to God. And the peace of God [that peace which reassures the heart, that peace] which transcends all understanding, [that peace which] stands guard over your hearts and your minds in Christ Jesus [is yours].

Index of Topics

More Books by this author

Ideas on How to Talk to the Boss

Ideas

This book offers simple strategies for Bible study, prayer, and growing your faith. Whether you're a beginner or experienced, it's a supportive guide to help you discover truth in God's Word.

Scan QR code here or go to:
https://bit.ly/3CEeRBD

Ideas on How to Talk to the Boss

Idea Book and Study Guide

This guide makes Bible study easy with practical methods and a 20-week plan of daily exercises. Whether you're new or experienced, you'll find ways to grow your relationship with the Lord.

Scan QR code here or go to:
https://bit.ly/3PWyzYb

Scan QR code

Little Prayers for Big Feelings

How kids use prayer to navigate through emotions

Little Prayers for Big Feelings helps kids tackle emotions with Bible-based prayers. Kids can tackle feelings like fear, sadness, and anger with confidence!

About the Author

Cynthia Radtke, a snow-loving M&M fanatic, is dedicated to teaching scripture to all ages and showing how to sneak it into everyday life, just like her favorite candy.

With 20+ years of teaching under her belt and plenty of stories as a foster parent, Cynthia has seen firsthand the value of children understanding and having a resource to help them deal with emotions and life's ups and downs. She has a heart dedicated to teaching God's Word to all ages; to cement it as a foundational component in their lives.

With a husband who keeps her laughing, Cynthia is always ready for the next unexpected twist!

For more books and insights, visit **travelmeetsfaith.com**

I've got something special just for you—a
"Why Should I?"
sheet that knocks out all those false accusations
with Biblical truth!

Just scan here:

Your voice is everything!

If this devotional helped you grow in your time with God, made the Bible feel easier to understand, or if the songs added a little extra bounce to your day, I'd love to hear about it!

Your feedback is like a little spark of encouragement for me and other girls on this journey.

www.ingramcontent.com/pod-product-compliance
Lightning Source LLC
Chambersburg PA
CBHW071300130626
46556CB00003B/1406